The Complete Love Circle

A Bible Study

By: Jane Wheeler

Published by: Ray of Sunshine Ministries

ISBN: 978-0-9958647-1-9 Softcover
ISBN: 978-0-9958647-3-3 ebook

Cataloguing Data Available From Library and Archives Canada

Scripture quotations are taken from The Holy Bible,
New International Version © 1973,1978,1984
By International Bible Society.
Used by Permission from Zondervan Publishing House

Published by: Ray of Sunshine Ministries

To Order Additional Copies Contact:
www.rayofsunshineministries.com

Other Books By Jane Wheeler

It Is Finished "Tetelestai": *The Most Powerful Words Ever Spoken*

ISBN
978-1-4602-1697-2 (Hardcover)
978-1-4602-1698-9 (Paperback)

Free To Fly

ISBN
978-1-4602-1705-4 (Hardcover)
978-1-4602-1706-1 (Paperback)

Midweek Moments 2016 Blog Posts of Jane Wheeler

ISBN
978-0-9958647-0-2

Dedication

This book is lovingly dedicated to my Mom.

A mother's love is something that we often take for granted.

No one else can really love you like your Mom.

My Mom went from being a Mom to also being a Friend.

Thank you Mom for all the lessons you taught me, the calm

presence when I needed it, the listening ear or shoulder to

cry on and most of all for showing me Love always.

I love you.

"For God so loved the world that he gave his one and only Son, that whoever believes in him shall not perish but have eternal life."

John 3:16

Table of Contents

Bible Studies are never meant to do the work for you. A true Bible study makes you "study" the Bible to think for yourself and glean new revelations that fuel your curiosity to make you dig deeper.

This book is designed to be used as an individual study but can also be used easily in a group setting.

Drawing Pages or Notes: You will find blank pages at the end of each chapter and at the end of the book that you can use to draw, doodle or create as God leads you. We each learn in our own way and some of us are visual and get pictures and others of us have to take notes.

Song: Music has a way of invading your soul. At the end of each chapter is a recommended "End Song", take the time to find the song and sit back and listen while meditating on what you learned in the chapter. Chapters 6 & 7 have both an end and beginning song to set the mood and prepare your hearts for the chapter.

Prayer: Prayer points are listed that you can use to guide you into time with God. These prayer times can be done individually or in a group but please take the time to do them. God is waiting to speak to each of you, let Him.

This book has been written with an ***Assumption***.

That assumption is that you the reader already have a relationship with the God of this Universe. This God is made up of three distinct persons, known as the Trinity: Father, Son – Jesus, Holy Spirit. If this statement has you questioning what I am talking about, then I need to explain. God created people to have a relationship with Him; that is the whole purpose of our existence. God has made Himself known to the world since the creation of time in one of those above three forms.

To have a relationship with God we need to look at how God says to do that.

"Jesus answered and said to him, 'Most assuredly I say to you, unless one is born again, he cannot see the kingdom of God.'"
John 3:3

The term "born again" is not a second physical birth, but rather a spiritual birth. It is the day you decide to have a relationship with God.

"Jesus answered, "I am the way and the truth and the life. No one comes to the Father except through me." John 14:6

Adam and Eve were created with this direct relationship to God, and when they were banished from the garden, this direct relationship to God was severed for all people. But God made a way back and that way is through Jesus, He said so. Jesus Christ died on the cross to do two things:

1. Restore this relationship with God
2. Jesus took on the sins of the world, yours and mine, because He loved us

To have a direct relationship with God requires that we acknowledge that Jesus Christ died for our sins. We all have sins, human nature is born with it, you do not have to teach children to lie or misbehave, it comes naturally.

Jesus said when He was taken up to heaven that He would not leave us alone, He would send us the Holy Spirit.

"... And I will ask the Father, and he will give you another advocate to help you and be with you forever— the Spirit of truth. The world cannot accept him, because it neither sees him nor knows him. But you know him, for he lives with you and will be in you." John 14:15-17

The Holy Spirit comes to live inside of us at our invitation, God will not force us, He is waiting for us to invite Him. This would be our second birth or spiritual birth otherwise known as "born again."

If you want to have this amazing relationship with God, it is simple, but only because it cost God so much (the life of Jesus), pray the following prayer: "God, I want to have a special relationship with you, I want you to be in my life. I acknowledge that Jesus paid for my sins when He died on the cross and I am ever grateful. I recognize that I cannot ever be good enough to get to heaven on my own, and I am totally blown away that you loved me and died for me even when I am not perfect. You love me just as I am. I invite you to come into my life. Please send your Holy Spirit to come and live inside of me, to share life with me, that I might never be separated from you again. I ask You to guide and teach me as we grow together. Thank you. Amen."

If you prayed this prayer, welcome to the "family". You are now a member of the family of God often known as a "Christian" – a follower of Jesus Christ.

Session 1: Imitation Versus Real

The Pearl Story:

A little girl, 4 years old out shopping with her mom at the local department store. They got near the checkout area which was filled with various kinds of kids treasures and candy placed at eye level to draw all children's attention.

The little 4 year old spotted a plastic pearl necklace hanging right in front of her face.

"Ohhh, can I get this mommy? Please can I get this?" she exclaims.

"Not today honey," Mommy answered, placing her groceries up onto the conveyor belt.

"But I love it. Please mommy, pl...ease!"

"Not today mommy said."

"I want it Mommy please!"

"Tell you what," Mommy countered back, "why don't we leave it today, and you can do some jobs around the house and earn the money to buy it. When you have enough money saved, we can come back and buy it. Okay?"

Sadly the little girl looked longingly at the pearls but nodded her okay with her head.

The little girl worked hard around the house and earned the money for the pearls in 3 weeks. They went back to the store to purchase the plastic pearl necklace.

True to her word the little girl "loved" the necklace and wore her plastic pearls every day. Faithfully every night she would slide them off her neck and carefully place them beside her bed before she went to sleep.

Daddy would come in and say prayers with her and kiss her good night. One night daddy said to her, "Honey, would you give Daddy your pearls?"

Shocked at the question the little girl wide eyed with amazement just shook her head and answered, "No Daddy, oh no!"

Daddy just smiled and kissed her good night saying, "That's okay honey. Have a good sleep."

Every night Daddy came in to say good night and at least once a week he would throw out the same question, "Honey would you give Daddy your pearls?"

Each time the answer was the same. This continued on for about 2 months.

One night Daddy came into the bedroom and the little girl was sitting on her bed sobbing.

"Honey what is the matter?" Daddy rushed over to her concerned.

"Ohhhh Daddy..... here," the little girl choked out amidst the sobs, she thrust out her little hands and lifted up her pearl necklace to give to her treasured possession to her Daddy.

What the little girl did not see was that each time Daddy asked her if he could have her pearls, his left hand always slid into his pocket on his pants. Tonight as Daddy reached out with his right hand to take the offered up plastic pearls, his left hand came out of the pocket with a small but long and slender box that had been in his pocket each night he came into say good night.

"Honey," Daddy said, "Daddy loves you so much, I never wanted you to have plastic pearls, you are much too precious to me, I want you to have "real" pearls," and he placed the new box with the new and precious pearl necklace into her hands.

❖

Authors' Story: That little girl was me in a way, except I was not so little. I had been walking down a road that was not the right path, I had wandered off course. God had taken me very quickly to Atlanta Georgia to attend a course that I thought I was going to learn to help other people with.

That is the funny thing: we often do not know how bad off we are unless God shines His light on an area, He gets out a bullhorn and yells, "Maybe we should take a look at this?" Even then He gives us the option to say, "No, I think I would rather not".

I had been saying "no" a lot to God and gradually God withdrew things I had thought I had "needed": people, my family, my church, my job until He got me to a place of isolation and He whisked me off to Georgia to reshape my thinking.

I had been substituting **my** choices, **my** plastic pearls into my life thinking they were the "real" thing. I had been on my own after my divorce and I was lonely, needy and wanting something more in my life so I was out there looking. But God, God wanted me to have only the real, precious and priceless treasures that He had stored up and were waiting for me.

*God **never** has plastic for us, **never** the imitation, He has true treasures and He is waiting to give them to us.*

Write here what you think some plastic imitations could be or use the pages at the end of the chapter to draw a picture if God gives you one.

REAL/TRUE	IMMITATION/PLASTIC

REAL/TRUE	IMMITATION/PLASTIC

Plastic Versus Real:

Church: this can be a plastic imitation when we chose where we will go to church based on our feelings and likes, or we can let God choose = real treasure. How many times do we say, "well I do not like the way they do (you fill in the blank)....."or "so and so hurt me so I will not go there..." We see it as an open sign to leave and go elsewhere. Have we truly prayed about which church God wants us in and what role or gifts He would have us use at that church?

Friends: when we choose our friends, are we choosing treasures, those who will sharpen us, keep us accountable = real treasures. Or do we choose friends who will sympathize with us, feel sorry with us, let us wallow in our messes = plastic imitation. We should all have a healthy balance of Christian and non-Christian friends but for our spiritual health and well-being we need to have solid Christian friends who will help keep us accountable.

Job: we long to do that one career that will fulfill us, and we head straight for it = plastic imitation. Have we asked Gods advice or counsel and gone with His advice on a career to get a real treasure for a job?

Death: this one took me by surprise when God added it to the list. Satan longs to taunt us with the thoughts that life is too hard = plastic imitation. Perhaps we ponder thoughts of, if we could just escape for a while or maybe we want to end our life to end the pain = plastic imitation. We lose sight that there is no death, we go from life to life, God promised us "eternal life" (eternal has no end) = real treasure.

*Optional: Additional Study on Death: see the following scriptures: Psalm 129:23-24, John 3:16, John 3:36, John 4:14, John 5:24, John 6:51, John 10:10, John 10:27-30, John 11:25-26, John 17:3, Romans 5:21, 2 Corinthians 4:17-18,1 Timothy 6:12, 1 John 2:17, 1 John 5:11-13, 1 John 5:20

Love: there are many things we can have in our lives that are plastic imitations but the most precious, the most costly and ***the one that is most counterfeited is LOVE.*** For everything that God has, satan has a counterfeit and he loves to fool us with plastic imitation. God tells us over and over in the Bible that God is Love. This means His whole personhood defines "love", the true complete and precious kind of love never the plastic.

"...God is Love" — that is who He is and it cannot change because God cannot change. 1 John 4:8

"So we have come to know and to believe the love that God has for us. God is love, and whoever abides in love abides in God, and God abides in him." 1 John 4:16

"For I [am] the LORD, I change not..." Malachi 3:6a

"I am Alpha and Omega, the beginning and the end, saith the Lord, which is, and which was, and which is to come, the Almighty."
Revelation 1:8 KJV

God is the most complete and perfect form of Love. The most sought after thing in the entire universe is Love. We were born to be loved. God wired that need into our bodies. Watch a new born baby snuggle in the arms of its mother and settle right down, that needy craving for love is found in that snuggle. But yet that is not even the kind of Love that God has for us. He has a complete, unconditional love that we cannot understand in our human form.

Write your description of "love" here:

The Bibles' version of love is probably different than yours, and because it is the most counterfeited, it is worth studying:

*"Dear friends, let us love one another, for love comes from God. Everyone who loves has been born of God and knows God. Whoever does not love does not know God, because **God is love**. This is how **God showed his love** among us: **He sent his one and only Son** into the world that we might live through him. This is love: not that we loved God, but **that he loved us** and sent his Son as an atoning sacrifice for our sins. Dear friends, **since God so loved***

*us, we also ought to love one another. No one has ever seen God; but if we love one another, **God lives in us and his love is made complete in us.**"* 1 John 4:7-12

*"This is how we know that we live in him and he in us: He has given us of his Spirit. And we have seen and testify that the Father has sent his Son to be the Savior of the world. If anyone acknowledges that Jesus is the Son of God, God lives in them and they in God. And so we know and rely on the love God has for us. **God is love**. Whoever lives in love lives in God, and God in them. This is how love is made complete among us so that we will have confidence on the day of judgment: In this world we are like Jesus. There is no fear in love. But perfect love drives out fear, because fear has to do with punishment. The one who fears is not made perfect in love."* 1 John 4:13-18

We tend to think that love is a gushy warm feeling, an emotion but in reality it is anything but. The following famous scripture is often read at weddings, those romantic, sentimental times, but upon closer inspection love is more than "feelings":

"Love is patient, love is kind. It does not envy, it does not boast, it is not proud. It does not dishonor others, it is not self-seeking, it is not easily angered, it keeps no record of wrongs. Love does not delight in evil but rejoices with the truth. It always protects, always trusts, always hopes, always perseveres. Love never fails." 1 Corinthians 13:4-8

Love is - 1 Corinthians 13:4-8 (16 pieces)

Always Hopes

Always Perseveres

Never Fails
Patient
Kind
Does Not Envy
Does Not Boast
Not Proud or Arrogant
Not Rude
Not Self Seeking
Not Easily Angered
No Record of Wrongs
Does Not Delight in Evil
Rejoices with the Truth
Always Protects
Always Trusts

© 2016 Jane Wheeler

1 Corinthians 13 lists 16 pieces or components of love. We tend to divide them up: "Well I do not keep a record of wrongs" or "I do not get easily angered ..."

But the truth of the matter is you cannot divide these love characteristics up because ALL of these things combined equals true love. *God is LOVE – He is ALL of these things – all components, not better at some parts than others. All of them equal. Complete Love, that is who God is, that is His character and He cannot change.*

Try to grasp that concept – it will become vitally important in this study. God is ALL 16 pieces – you cannot take any away or divide them up.

This is the way God loves us, the way He loves you. Put your name into the above circle and say each segment with your name attached. Example: God does not remember (your name's) wrongs. God is not easily angered by (your name). God never fails (your name). Keep going until you have inserted your name into all 16 segments.

Write what you feel when you do that:

Do you believe this is true?

One of the most important lessons I learned in Georgia was on love. You see, as with pearls, you cannot tell imitation pearls or imitation love, from the real pearls or real love, unless you are an expert.

Teaching Demo*:* have a plastic pearl bracelet or necklace and compare it to a real pearl bracelet or necklace. From a distance you cannot tell the difference.

Imitations can fool most people but God wants us to know "real love" because "real love equals God".

"***God is Love."*** 1 John 4:8

The only love worth our time and attention to learn about is Gods' love; if we think our small heartfelt feelings are "love" we will learn we are way off base. As a matter of fact it is "prideful" to even think we are capable of loving others or even ourselves with the right kind of "love".

4 Different Kinds of Love in Greek language:

eros, storge, phileo, agape

Eros – root of our word "erotic", named after the Greek god of fertility – a sexual, passionate love. This word is not used in the Bible.

Storge - the love and affection that naturally occurs between parents and children and can exist between siblings.

Phileo/Philia - to have a special interest in someone or something, frequently with focus on close association; have affection for, to like, consider someone a friend.   example: I love my car or I love ice cream

Agape - is the very nature of God, for God is love. The key to understanding *agape* is to realize that it can be known from the action it prompts, not the feelings. God so "loved" (*agape*) the world that He gave His Son. It did not feel good to God to do that, but it was the loving thing to do (action). Christ so loved (*agape*) the world that He gave His life.

 Agape love is an exercise of the will, a deliberate choice. This is why God can command us to love our enemies (Matthew 5:44; Exodus 23:1-5). He is not commanding us to "have a good feeling" for our enemies, but to act in a loving way toward them. "Loving" someone is to obey God on another's behalf, seeking his or her long-term blessing and profit; it can be hard and feel unpleasant. Another component of agape love is discipline. We love our children and we discipline them for their "good". Sometimes we have to say no or draw boundaries for the good of the other person, but always this is to be done in love. Actions then are the signs of love, not feelings.

In John 21:15-17 Watch the difference between *agape* and *phileo* in the following passage:

Jesus: Simon...do you love (*agape*) me more than these?

Peter: Yes, Lord; you know that I love (*phileo*) you.

Jesus: Simon...do you...love (*agape*) me?

Peter: Yes, Lord, you know that I love (*phileo*) you.

Jesus: Simon...do you love (*phileo*) me?

Peter: [Grieved] "Lord...you know that I love (*phileo*) you."

Go back to the 4 Love definitions and write down the difference in the words for "love" in the above conversation? Write it out here:

Why did you think Jesus uses *agape* and Peter use *phileo*?

Jesus was asking Peter if he loved him with the love of God, a love that may require sacrifice. Jesus had just gone through a horrendous crucifixion for Peter's sake (and ours), something He did not want to do but He did it anyway because of His *agape* love. In contrast, Peter had avoided possible torture by denying Jesus three times the night before the crucifixion.

Jesus twice asked Peter, "Do you *agape* me?" (He was essentially asking: are you willing to do things for me that you do not want to do?) Peter was not sure so he was letting Jesus know that he was still a true friend, and had *phileo* love, best friend love, for Jesus.

The third time Jesus spoke to Peter, He asked if Peter were indeed a true friend (*phileo*), which hurt Peter. Jesus knew what Peter did not know, that Jesus would be taken up into heaven, and Peter and the others would be left to carry out his work on earth. Work that would require that they do His will even when it meant it would be hard.

Filters: Almost all of us were raised in some kind of home with some kind of adult parent or guardian watching over us. Those homes, those early memories are what shaped our thinking of "love", those are our "filters". How we were treated or loved is how we will probably love others. Peter had a filter and he weighed his commitment to Jesus in the above conversation by his own previous actions of denying Jesus in the courtyard before the crucifixion. (Luke 22:54-62, Mark 14:66-72, John 18:15-27)

Gods' original design was to give us parents to teach us about love, family and responsibilities but some families did not do well in this area; actually, **ALL** families mess up in some way or another in this area. Why? Because **ALL** families are composed of imperfect people, there is no person in this world who is perfect, the Bible says:

"for there is no distinction; for all have sinned and fall short of the glory of God." Romans 3:22-23

The result is that each one of us has a different "filter" on what love and family should look like. This is why marriage can be so difficult, two totally different opinions or "filters" trying to mesh as one. You might want to keep your children from experiencing pain in their childhood by trying to be the perfect parent or grandparent. The truth is, you will not be able to. We all will mess up along the way.

Teaching Demo Part 1: take a clear glass of water

If Gods perfect love is clean and refreshing, satisfying deep into our souls it would look like this: clear perfect water.

Teaching Demo Part 2: Have some sand or dirt. Put the dirt or sand into a tea strainer (fine strainer) and pour the clear water through the sand/dirt to show cloudy, muddy water.

Our hearts represented by the sand/dirt are years of what we were shown **love is** whether or not you think it was good or bad it still gave you a filter. You will grow up seeing God and love through your filter the way it was taught to you. The muddy water is our filter, even with God's pure love inside us.

After we become a Christian, if you have invited God's Holy Spirit to come and live inside of you, God's pure love gets placed inside of us: *"that is the Spirit of truth, whom the world cannot receive, because it does not see Him or know Him, but you know Him because He abides with you and will be in you."*   John 14:17

"Or do you not know that your body is a temple of the Holy Spirit who is in you, whom you have from God, and that you are not your own?"   1 Corinthians 6:19

From our demo, we see that when we pour the clean pure love, Gods' love, into our filtered hearts, we get a muddied looking love in our life, showing us what **we** think love should look like.

We may be absolutely certain in our minds and hearts that the way we love is right because it feels right, but unless we truly know what pure love is without our filters, how do we know if our love is muddied or not?

Write your thoughts on filtered love here:

What could be some of the consequences of having filtered love?

We will spend the next few weeks studying the ramifications of what substituting our imitation or muddied love could be: the plastic versus the real.

1) Separation from God and His Word, His Person and His Love.

2) Separation from Self – not accepting yourself, not loving yourself, condemnation

3) Separation from Others – hatred, bitterness, jealousy, competition, broken relationships

Love affects everything because your whole life hinges on "Love" - Gods' two great commandments:

"Jesus replied: 'Love the Lord your God with all your heart and with all your soul and with all your mind.' This is the first and greatest commandment. And the second is like it: Love your neighbor as yourself.' All the Law and the Prophets hang on these two commandments."   Matthew 22:37-40

End with Song: *Your Love Never Fails* by Jesus Culture

Prayer Time: Take some time to think of Love as taught in 1 Corinthians 13:4-8. Ask God to show you if you believe He is complete love in all 16 areas or are there some pieces you are unsure about, areas where you have doubts. Confess those doubts to God and repent of putting 'your' version of God's love ahead of His.

Drawings, Doodles & Notes:

Drawings, Doodles & Notes:

Session 2: Separation from God, Who's Your Daddy?

Recap: Session 1 Imitation Versus Real Love, Plastic versus Real

Open with Story: *My Daddy's Pantry* by Jane Wheeler
Published on Midweek Moments Blog April 13, 2016

I was reminded recently of an activity that when I was able to do this – brought me much delight. Someone talked about going "home" back to our parents of origin's actual home and how when we got there things changed. It was the one place on earth where you were free to look into the cupboards and check out what was new without being reprimanded or being accused of being "snoopy" or "rude". I would never think of going into other people's cupboards or snooping around their homes.

Home was the safe place you knew that what Mom and Dad had was yours. If I needed a tool for a project, I asked Dad if I could borrow the saw for a couple days and walked right into the workshop and got it. If I needed some sewing or craft supplies, I would ask mom if she had any bright yellow buttons and walk right into her sewing room and look around to find what she had. What my mom and dad had they shared with me. I now love to share what I have my boys as well.

Then there was my favorite and both my sister and I loved it – we would always go to the food cupboard or pantry where mom kept the "good stuff". That was where we tried the new snack bars from Costco or found the stash of Werther's butterscotch candies or chocolate bars. Mom was so awesome at always having some good stuff on hand in that cupboard and she rarely let us down.

Now that Dad is gone and Mom is in a home with Alzheimer's, we fill moms' little fridge with "good stuff". I often wonder if she gets

as delighted as us when she goes into the fridge to find the treasures waiting in there.

I am challenged when I pray to stop and think about who I am praying to. Am I praying and reciting the same words over and over or am I excited to pray brand new everyday with fresh joy and excitement. Do I pray with the same excitement as going into my parents' house?

I shut my eyes and tried to think of walking into Gods house the same as walking into mom and dads' and I got a picture in my mind.

As I pray now, I picture myself walking right into a huge stock filled pantry of my Daddy's house. I am not an orphan who just hopes my prayers go somewhere and get answered - I am a child of God. The God of this universe who has storehouses I cannot even imagine and He wants to share with me. So now as I pray I picture myself pulling the item off the panty shelf and placing them into my arms because whatever my Daddy has He is more than willing to share with me and man does He have some "good stuff".

❖

Do you get excited to go to your earthly parents' house?

Depending on how you answer that question could filter how you approach your Heavenly Fathers house.

Think about this: before you were a son/daughter, a brother/sister, a friend, a husband/wife or a dad/mom; **you were a Child of God**. This is how you were born into this world as <u>a child of the most high King</u>, this **is** <u>your true identity</u> and you have a Heavenly Daddy.

Have you ever had your earthly Daddy tell you that he loved you?

Repeatedly in small or large crowds the answer to this question is fairly consistent. Over 80% of people have never had their earthly Daddy tell them that he loved them. You may have felt loved but if you never actually heard the words it has created a void or a filter in your life.

God has chosen to both tell us **verbally**, with words, and secondly, He **showed us** His love by sending His Son to die for us. If God thought it was important to do both, verbally tell us as well as show us His love, it should be important for us to do both with our children.

If you do not or did not trust your Daddy on earth chances are you will not trust your Daddy in heaven. We have a filter, remember the muddied water from the demo in chapter 1?

Think back to your earthly daddy.

Were you ever afraid of him? Why?

Did you run to him with everything that happened to you?

Did he always protect you?

Your earthly daddy may have been wonderful but he was not perfect OR your earthly daddy may have been harsh and unyielding. We all have some behaviors in our head that we would not do if our earthly daddy's were around us. A daddy's presence can alter our behavior: for both our earthly and heavenly father. We all have a filter when it comes to our fathers.

Filters from our past create a block in our heart and because of these it is impossible to feel 100% of our heavenly Fathers love. This is called *separation from God*.

Because of a lack of Father's love, boys and girls, you and me, we learn to look for love in all the wrong places. We have tried to fill the void with a variety of things clutching for some kind of life preserver to make us feel "loved". This is true in our earthly relationship with our dads and also in our relationship with our heavenly dad.

Earthly Dad: Remember we have a built in love tank that needs filled, without our earthly father's love this can be a reason peer pressure is huge and powerful over our young people. Gangs have a pull because in a gang you can "belong" and be "accepted". Sports teams can become our home and coaches can replace our dads. Churches can become our family and pastors can represent our dads. Girls often look for boyfriends or men who will give her the love her heart is so desperate for. Focus on the Family[1] has some great programs that explain that a girl/woman who grows up not knowing that she was loved, accepted and

---

[1] Focus On The Family Link to Website: https://www.focusonthefamily.ca

beautiful to her father will attempt to find that love, acceptance and affirmation elsewhere. She may become promiscuous because finally a man is showing her "love" (plastic).

Wherever there is a lack in any of the love "segments", remember the 16 pieces, people will attempt to find someone or something that can rescue them from this feeling of being "unloved."

Heavenly Dad: if we do not feel loved by our heavenly Father it can cause us to look in the wrong places as well. People tend to become "doers". Example: I will prove that I am worth loving and I become a "super" Christian. Control: if I do not feel completely loved I may take on "control" issues. Groupie: I can start looking to pastors or Bible teachers, work members, bosses as father type figures.

Before you can love God or accept His love for you, you have to know who He is, without our old filters getting in the way.

Is our heavenly Father trust worthy? Write your thoughts here:

Just what would a perfect Daddy look like to you? Allow yourself to go back in your mind to your childhood, write your thoughts:

I did up a Daddy Job Description. I went back into my little girls' heart and thought about what would be a perfect daddy.

My Daddy Job Description

The following is the list my Bible study class and I came up with.

My Daddy has to: Love Me, Protect Me, Be Strong, Provide For Me, Always Be There, Rescue Me, Teach Me, Discipline Me, Must Be Able to Fix Things, Exterminate All Spiders and Bugs, Make Me Laugh, Be Willing to Die for Me.

Group note: there is a lot of scripture listed here, pick 2-3 scriptures per item and get people in the class to read them out.

My Daddy Has to Love Me:

Deuteronomy 7:9

Palm 62:12

Psalm 86:15

Proverbs 8:17

Jeremiah 31:3

Zephaniah 3:17

Romans 8:37-39

My Daddy Has to Protect Me:

Deuteronomy 10:17-18

2 Samuel 22:3-4

Psalm 4:8

Psalm 5:11

Psalm 138:7

Proverbs 30:5

1 Corinthians 13:7

My Daddy Has To Be Strong:

Deuteronomy 3:24

Psalm 24:8

Psalm 62:11

1 Corinthians 1:25

My Daddy Has To Provide For Me:

Job 38:41

Psalm 34:10

Matthew 6:31-32

Luke 12:24

1 Corinthians 10:13

Philippians 4:19

My Daddy Has To Always Be There:

Deuteronomy 31:6

Joshua 1:5-6, 9

Isaiah 41:10

Matthew 28:20

Romans 8:38-39

My Daddy Has To Be Able To Rescue Me:

1 Samuel 7:8

2 Chronicles 20:15

Psalm 22:4-5

Psalm 43:1

Psalm 107:19

Psalm 121

Proverbs 18:10

Jeremiah 20:13

Hebrews 13:6

My Daddy Has To Teach & Lead Me:

Exodus 4:15

Psalm 25:12

Psalm 32:8

Jeremiah 32:33

Micah 4:2

John 16:13-15 spirit of truth

2 Timothy 3:16-17

James 1:5

My Daddy Has To Discipline Me:

Deuteronomy 8:5

Proverbs 3:12

Hebrews 12:5-8

Revelation 3:19

My Daddy Must Be Able to Fix Things:

Genesis 18:14

Jeremiah 32:27

Mark 5:36-42

Luke 18:27

Feeding of the 5,000 (15,000) – Matthew 14:13-21, Mark 6:30-44, Luke 9:10-17; John 6:1-14

My Daddy Has To Exterminate All Spiders and Bugs and Things that Bump in the Night:

1 Samuel 17:4 –9, 45-47 David and Goliath

My Daddy Has To Make Me Laugh: Creation

Proverbs 11:22

Proverbs 15:13

My Daddy Has Be Willing to Die For Me:

Isaiah 53:5

Matthew 20:28

John 1:29

John 3:16-17

1 Corinthians 15:22

1 John 3:16

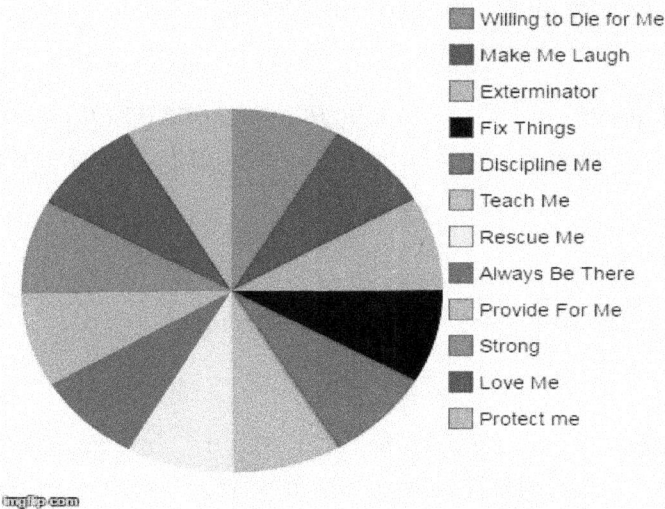

Daddy Job Description

- Willing to Die for Me
- Make Me Laugh
- Exterminator
- Fix Things
- Discipline Me
- Teach Me
- Rescue Me
- Always Be There
- Provide For Me
- Strong
- Love Me
- Protect me

© 2016 Jane Wheeler

My Daddy has to: Love Me, Protect Me, Be Strong, Provide For Me, Always Be There, Rescue Me, Teach Me, Discipline Me, Must Be Able to Fix Things, Exterminate All Spiders and Bugs, Make Me Laugh, Be Willing to Die for Me.

Just like the love circle, the Daddy circle is a complete unit, no one segment can be taken out or removed. God as our Daddy is one Daddy made up of many sections. In our minds we try to divide Him up. Example: I believe He will guide and teach me but do I believe He will provide for me?

Nope, stop that! You cannot do that, you cannot separate the segments He is one complete unit, you cannot divide Him up. When we divide the segments we are actually agreeing and saying to ourselves, that God is not able to do that. We believe that His ability to be our heavenly daddy is plastic or imitation, not a true jewel and remember He does not want you to have plastic.

God Loves You! He sent His Son to die in your place, He saved and protected you. He thinks the world of you and He wants you to know how special you are to Him. We need to re-program our thinking into God thinking.

"For God so loved the world that he gave his one and only Son, that whoever believes in him shall not perish but have eternal life."
John 3:16

End Song: *Good Good Father by Chris Tomlin*

Prayer Time: Spend some time reflecting on your earthly father. Do you need to forgive Him for thinking He failed you in some of the Daddy Job Description areas? Ask God to show you where you have doubts or filters about God's Daddy abilities. Confess those doubts and ask God to forgive you. Ask God to give you a fresh new revelation of His love for you.

Drawings, Doodles & Notes:

Drawings, Doodles & Notes:

Session 3: Who You Are To God

Recap

Session 1 Imitation Versus Real Love, Filtered versus Real Love
Gods' pure love = 16 segments of 1 Corinthians 13:4-8
Session 2 Separation From God. Who's Your Daddy? – Daddy Job
Description, God is all segments, cannot separate

❖

Open with Story: Chapter 1 Fairy Tales and Reality[2]

You gather your mail and are surprised as you sift through the endless flyers and bulk "for occupant" mail to see a rather elegant gold metallic envelope in the pile. Your name is written in perfect calligraphic script; curious, you re-check the name. Yes, it is for you. Pleasantly surprised, you expectantly tear and rip it open.

Oh! An invitation.

God has extended an invitation to you to come and meet with Him. He wants to express His love for you and has a gift to give you. Totally overwhelmed, you question this, mulling and swirling dozens of thoughts at one time around in your mind, for who are you to be invited into the presence of the King, yet alone be given a gift? Who are you that you should be noticed?

You wonder if you should go, yet you know that you will. You begin to ponder the preparations in your mind. What should you wear? (The question never changes down through the ages!) You decide it has to be something new, something special, something that will make you look...not plain, for that is the way you feel inside: plain, ordinary, nothing special. The outfit will make the difference!

---

[2] *Free To Fly*, Jane Wheeler Chapter 1: Fairy Tales and Reality

And yet, deep down, you know the outfit will not change anything; you will still be the same ordinary person you know you are.

You wonder if the invitation was really for you or was there a mix-up in the guest list.

On the day of the appointment, you spend your time primping and fussing until at last, with an exasperated sigh, you conclude there is not much else you can do with yourself; it is as good as it gets, and you go.

You approach the door of the royal palace with tremors in your legs and butterflies in your stomach. The messenger who answers greets you in a fine and royal manner as if he was expecting to see you. He announces that the King is waiting for you and that you are to go right in as He is expecting you. Startled and looking around you ask if the other guests have arrived, and are even more startled as he tells you that you are to be the only guest.

He leads you into the great room—not just any room, but a radiant room. The elegant, exquisite décor are such that you gasp upon entering such a fine room. You warily glance about the room, sweeping it with your eyes shaking off the feeling like you should not be here. Then you notice it—the light at the end of the room, a light unlike any other, a warm, comforting light; it seems to beckon you.

As you approach the end of the room, you notice the light is being emitted from a figure, a figure seated on a throne; it is the figure of the King.

The fear and tremors that have been taunting you have ceased and all that you feel now is the compelling warmth, emanating from this figure. You approach slowly and then bow down very low to the floor and expectantly wait.

Suddenly you feel the presence of a hand upon your shoulder, and you look up, up into eyes that you have never experienced before. You see eyes that portray only warmth, compassion, and something that you cannot imagine that would be there for you: love. You fluster and start to explain your presence, saying how quite fine it is with you if there was a mix-up in the invitation, for you do not really know why you got invited; you could leave and would not be offended.

The radiant face just beams down at you. Gently, so very gently, He lifts your head up, cradling your face between both His warm, strong hands. With a voice oh so tender, He says: "My child, there has been no mix-up. I have been waiting for you. I have longed to meet with you many times, but you were too busy to come and dismissed my many messengers when they came with my invitation. I have longed to show you my Kingdom and to share my Kingdom with you. I have sent my messengers out many times. When my messengers would go out, I would wait by the gate to see if you had accepted my invitations, but always, always, they returned disheartened.

But now you are here, and we have the time to get to know each other better. I have kept watch over you since the day you were born—in fact, I was at your birth and I even saw you when you were in your mother's womb. Oh, my child, you are more beautiful with each passing day; you have blossomed into a beautiful person. I was so right to give you those lovely eyes. But come, come my child, and talk with me, I so long to hear your voice and hear the longings of your heart. Come."

Hand in hand, you go to a place prepared for just two, and you talk, long, long into the night. He is so easy to talk to; He listens so intently as if you were His only thought in the world. His voice is alive with emotion, and His laugh—oh, His laugh!—it is indescribable.

Then it happens: He gets a look over His face that flashes just for an instant, quick but not quick enough for you not to notice. He tells in a voice so deep and raw with emotion a tale that catches you sharply, and you realize that as He speaks, you are holding your breath.

He tells you of an old and ancient enemy that has had spies come into the land to spy and scout out the Kingdom. This enemy has sent a letter—a ransom note—to the King, demanding that in order to preserve peace and not be overtaken in a violent and bloody war that a pact be signed. In sealing the Pact, a token must be given to ensure good faith on the King's part.

"The enemy has asked for you, my child, as a sign to seal the Pact." As the King is speaking, tears well up in His eyes, and then they just overflow, running in streams down His face. "Oh my child, I have searched my Kingdom over to see what I can do to take away this burden. My heart is heavy within me at the thought of ever losing you or anyone of my kingdom to this enemy. I fear if I do not release you to him he will come in the deep of night and whisk you away. I have been searching for the right gift to give to seal this pact—a gift that would not only express my love and affection for you and the others in my Kingdom, but one that would also satisfy the enemy. I know now what that gift must be: a gift that is

perfect, unflawed, one that is of the utmost value to me. Not money, nor fame, nor gold or precious gems. You see, my child, these things perish; no, my gift to him will be..."

There is total solemn silence, and when He speaks it is in a slow strained whisper: "...my Son—my own precious Son; the gift will be the Prince."

Can you feel the emotion?

God loves you and has done everything to save you from the hands of the enemy. He paid the ransom price for you. He is the personification of Agape love. It did not feel good, it was not mushy, it had emotion but it required action and sacrifice.

Read the Prodigal Son Story:

"Jesus continued: "There was a man who had two sons. The younger one said to his father, 'Father, give me my share of the estate.' So he divided his property between them.

"Not long after that, the younger son got together all he had, set off for a distant country and there squandered his wealth in wild living. After he had spent everything, there was a severe famine in that whole country, and he began to be in need. So he went and hired himself out to a citizen of that country, who sent him to his fields to feed pigs. He longed to fill his stomach with the pods that the pigs were eating, but no one gave him anything.

"When he came to his senses, he said, 'How many of my father's hired servants have food to spare, and here I am starving to death! I will set out and go back to my father and say to him: Father, I have sinned against heaven and against you. I am no

longer worthy to be called your son; make me like one of your hired servants.' So he got up and went to his father.

"But while he was still a long way off, his father saw him and was filled with compassion for him; he ran to his son, threw his arms around him and kissed him.

"The son said to him, 'Father, I have sinned against heaven and against you. I am no longer worthy to be called your son.'

"But the father said to his servants, 'Quick! Bring the best robe and put it on him. Put a ring on his finger and sandals on his feet. Bring the fattened calf and kill it. Let's have a feast and celebrate. For this son of mine was dead and is alive again; he was lost and is found.' So they began to celebrate."   Luke 15:11-32

Where was the father when the son came up the road? Underline it in the above passage. Why is this significant?[3]

How did the Father react when the son confessed his failings? Underline it in the passage.

---

[3] **Answer:** This is significant because the Father was always watching, he never gave up hope, he expected his son to return. The Father in the story is a representation of your Heavenly Father – He always waits for you to come home.

How would you react if your child came home after along presence away?

Your heavenly Father longs to have you come into His presence, you are one of His kids. God takes great delight in you.

"The Lord your God ...will take great delight in you, He will quiet you with His love, He will rejoice over you with singing."
Zephaniah 3:17

You are one of God's heirs.
Heir Definition: a person legally entitled to the property or rank of another on that person's death

"Now if we are children, then we are heirs - heirs of God and co-heirs with Christ, if indeed we share in his sufferings in order that we may also share in his glory." Romans 8:17

When God talks about you in heaven – did you know God talks about you in heaven? Hey you are one of His kids, He talks about you.

He has a special name He uses just for you. Do you believe that?

Thoughts:

Have you ever asked Him how He sees you? Ask Him to show you, write what comes to your mind here or draw a picture on the empty pages at the end of the chapter:

Names: the Bible talks of how important a name should be.

In the Bible a name is often a description of the person himself or herself or of what the parents would like their child to become. Every given name has a special meaning to go with it, for example the name Jane means precious gift of God.

God is also going to give you a new name – it says so in the book of Revelation.

"I will give him . . . a new name written on the stone which no one knows but he who receives it. . . . I will write on him the name of My God, and the name of the city of My God, the new Jerusalem, which comes down out of heaven from My God, and My new name." (Revelation 2:17; 3:12)

God knows you, He is going to use your new name to show you what His plans and heart holds for you.

Jesus gave Simon Peter a new name: *"You are Simon the son of John; you shall be called Cephas (which is translated Peter)."* John 1:42   Cephas means "rock"

God changed Abram and Sarai's names: Abram – exalted father, became Abraham – father of many or multitude. Sarai – princess, became Sarah - mother of nations. Genesis 17:5 and Genesis 17:15

Jacob – undermines or the heel, becomes Israel - he who struggles with God.   *"Your name will no longer be Jacob, but Israel, because you have struggled with God and with humans and have overcome."* Genesis 32:28

God, your heavenly Daddy, knows what His plans and purposes are for you, He has a name that is designed with you in mind. God knows <u>your</u> name, both your given and your "spiritual" name. This is how God thinks of you, this is how God talks about you and how you should be thinking of yourself.

God can speak to us in different ways, with His Word, visions, dreams, other people, and prophecy. Go back in your past and think of things people have said or prophetic words that have been spoken over you or even scriptures that really speak to your heart. Consider and pray and ask God if that is how He sees you. God created you with a purpose in mind, He will let you know what it is if you ask Him. Remember God's primary goal is to conform you into the image of His Son.

"For those God foreknew he also predestined to be conformed to the image of his Son, that he might be the firstborn among many brothers and sisters." Romans 8:29

God does not work on behavior; He works on your identity. God lets you know who you are to Him, and then He helps you to walk into that destiny planned especially for you.

Go back and look at the list of name changes and write what each new name means and what would it mean for that person's destiny. I have done the first one for you.

Old Name	Old Meaning	New Name	Destiny
Abram	exalted father	Abraham	father of many
Sarai			
Simon	listen		
Jacob			
Saul	asked for		little, humble
Your Name			
Mine: Jane	Precious Gift of God	Sunshine	Bring light to a dark world

I have aligned myself with God to walk forward knowing that it is one of my purposes to bring light to a dark world. I love it! It is who I am and who I was created to be, it is freeing to know this.

If you have not received your special name yet: it is okay. Ask Him and wait because God is faithful and will tell you; for now He has told us some special names of how He sees all of us and we can certainly use those.

You Are His **Beloved**

"Beloved, *we are now children of God, and what we will be has not yet been revealed. We know that when Christ appears, we will be like Him, for we will see Him as He is."* 1 John 3:2 KJV

"Beloved, *I wish above all things that thou mayest prosper and be in health, even as thy soul prospereth."* 3 John 1:2 KJV

"Put on therefore, as the elect of God, holy and **beloved**, *bowels of mercies, kindness, humbleness of mind, meekness, longsuffering;"* Colossians 3:12

There is truly a place of safety when you know that you are God's beloved. We are not being proud when we call ourselves God's beloved. It is not boastful when we know that it is God's grace that has made us accepted in the Beloved! We had nothing to do with it, our job is to accept it.

"To all who are **beloved** *of God in Rome, called as saints: Grace to you and peace from God our Father and the Lord Jesus Christ."* Romans 1:7

"Therefore, my **beloved** *brethren, be steadfast, immovable, always abounding in the work of the Lord, knowing that your toil is not in vain in the Lord."* 1 Corinthians 15:58

"Listen, my **beloved** *brethren: did not God choose the poor of this world to be rich in faith and heirs of the kingdom which He promised to those who love Him?"* James 2:5

"to the praise of the glory of His grace, by which He made us accepted in the **Beloved**.*"* Ephesians 1:6

Daughter/Son - children

God calls you His son and daughter, His child. Children belong to someone, they have rights to the family, you belong.

*"Yet to all who did receive him, to those who believed in his name, he gave the right to become **children of God**."* John 1:12

*"For those who are led by the Spirit of God are the **children of God**. The Spirit you received does not make you slaves, so that you live in fear again; rather, the Spirit you received brought about your adoption to **sonship**.[a] And by him we cry, "Abba, Father." The Spirit himself testifies with our spirit that **we are God's children**."*   Romans 8:14-16

You are **Predestined**

'Pre' meaning before: a long time ago before you were a Christian, before you were saved, before you even knew about God, HE chose you and handpicked you.

*"For those God foreknew he also **predestined** to be conformed to the image of his Son, that he might be the firstborn among many brothers and sisters. And those he **predestined**, he also called; those he called, he also justified; those he justified, he also glorified."* Romans 8:29-30

You Are **Chosen** By God

What an awesome concept, you are chosen by the God of this universe, He picked you!

*"And so, as those who have been **chosen** of God, holy and **beloved**, put on a heart of compassion, kindness, humility, gentleness and patience; bearing with one another, and forgiving each other, whoever has a complaint against anyone; just as the Lord forgave*

you, so also should you. And beyond all these things put on love, which is the perfect bond of unity." Colossians 3:12-17

Wonderful: You are fearfully and wonderfully made
Psalm 139:13-14

> *"For you created my inmost being;*
> *you knit me together in my mother's womb.*
> *I praise you because I am fearfully and wonderfully made;*
> *your works are wonderful,*
> *I know that full well."*

The Chosen of God

Notice the difference from **Chosen** to **The Chosen**. In the first you are chosen, picked out of the crowd. Now you are in the "group" the crowd belonging to God, forever identified with Him.

The Chosen: *eklektos,* Greek Word meaning "chosen out, select." It can also be translated as "elect" (*Vine's Expository Dictionary of Old and New Testament Words,*)

*"But we are bound to give thanks always to God for you, brethren beloved of the Lord, because God hath from the beginning **chosen** you to salvation through sanctification of the Spirit and belief of the truth: Whereunto he called you by our gospel, to the obtaining of the glory of our Lord Jesus Christ."* 2 Thessalonians 2:13-14

The Called _kletos - Greek Work is related to the noun *klesis*, which means "a calling" (*Vine's Expository Dictionary of Old and New Testament Words*)

It is important to understand that one's calling is an act of God! He calls (invites) you, we do not initiate it – God does. He sought you out and called you: chosen

Jesus tells the crowds, *"No one can come to Me unless the Father who sent Me draws him."* John 6:44

Activity:

Start to put your name into the names listed above:

(your name) the beloved son/daughter of God.

God has chosen (your name) to be His son/daughter.

(your name) is a child of God.

(your name) is wonderfully and perfectly made.

How does this feel to hear God say these things about you?

Write these phrases on index cards and put them into places where you will find them. Example: bathroom drawer, under your pillow, in the car...read them until you believe them.

End Song: *He Knows My Name* by Francesca Battistelli

Prayer: Ask God to show you how He sees you. Ask Him what plans, purposes He has for your life. Be open to any new ideas and thoughts and dreams He gives you.

Drawings, Doodles & Notes:

Drawings, Doodles & Notes:

Session 4: Separation from Self

Recap

Session 1 Imitation Versus Real Love – Plastic or Real Pearls

Session 2 Separation From God – Who's Your Daddy?

Session 3 Who You Are to God – He Knows Your Name

❖

What does it mean to be separated from yourself, what would the effects look like?

Write your thoughts here:

<u>Separation from Self</u> could have any of the following attributes:

Selfishness, unlovable, cranky, uncompassionate, hardened, do not like yourself, cannot look at yourself in the mirror, feelings of inferiority, suspicious, control, self-loathing, negative, critical, pessimistic. Sometimes the class clown is the person who does not love themselves - they are in constant need for approval and recognition from others. We judge them thinking they are so full of themselves, over confident, wanting to be the center of attention when just the opposite is true. Other people find it hard to love a person who does not love themselves, they can "pull you down", they take a lot of emotional energy to be around.

Not really the nicest of lists, is it?

We have been talking about our filters, why does it matter if we do not have the proper view of God?

Write here what filters create in our lives?[4]

"He answered, 'Love the Lord your God with all your heart and with all your soul and with all your strength and with all your mind'; and, 'Love your neighbor as yourself.'" Luke 10:27

Activity: Go back and re-read the above Luke 10:27 passage, underline the phrases: Love the Lord your God, Love you neighbor and as yourself.

God, Others, Self

I ask you now to consider how can you love God with ALL your heart and All your soul and All your strength and ALL your mind, if you really do not know what True love is? If we do not trust our Heavenly Father as our totally complete and trustworthy "Daddy" (circle graph) is this possible? Thoughts:

---

[4] Answer: They create one of three things: Separation from God, Self and Others

Remember God only wants true precious pearls for us, not imitation plastic. He wants us to have His complete undivided love (1 Corinthians 13). We cannot take pieces out, He is the complete and total circle.

If we have muddied love because in our past we had poor parenting, poor examples, hurts, abuse, broken trust, or betrayal, instead of clear pure love, how can we even know how to do this commandment?   And yet, God says to love Him with All our Hearts and Minds and Strength.

Is He asking us to do something that is impossible? Write your thoughts here:

"This is the covenant I will establish with the people of Israel after that time, declares the Lord. I will put my laws in their minds and write them on their hearts. I will be their God, and they will be my people." Hebrews 8:10

"This is the covenant I will make with them after that time, says the Lord. I will put my laws in their hearts, and I will write them on their minds." Hebrews 10:16

God knew beforehand that we would be unable to remember and keep His commands, so He said that **He will** write them and put them into our hearts and minds.

Activity: Underline the "I Wills" in the above 2 verses

He did much more than that; our Daddy thought of everything because He wants us to have the "real" thing not the imitation plastic. Remember in our complete Daddy job description (circle graph) our perfect Daddy would teach and instruct us, and He said He would provide for us. God knew that just reminding us of what to do would not be enough for His wandering people so He did something even more extreme. <u>He gave us the ability to have His laws written inside of us a continual reminder.</u>

Is this a new thought?

"Therefore say to the Israelites, 'This is what the Sovereign LORD says: It is not for your sake, people of Israel, that I am going to do these things, but for the sake of my holy name, which you have profaned among the nations where you have gone." Ezekiel 36:22

Activity/Answer: underline "for the sake of my holy name"

God says repeatedly in the Bible that He will not share His glory with another. It is for His glory that He did this.

"I am the LORD; that is my name! I will not yield my glory to another or my praise to idols." Isaiah 42:8

"For my own sake, for my own sake, I do this. How can I let myself be defamed? I will not yield my glory to another." Hebrews 48:11

God knew beforehand that mankind would not be able to live up to His standards so He took the steps to enable us to do it by giving us a New heart, a living pearl, not imitation plastic. He enabled the Holy Spirit, a piece of Himself to enter into us. By doing that, He not only wrote His commandments on our hearts and minds but He also gave us a NEW heart.

*"This is the covenant **I will** make with the house of Israel after that time,' declares the Lord. **'I will** put my law in their minds and write in on their hearts. **I will** be their God and they will be my people."* Jeremiah 31:33

*"They will be my people, and **I will** be their God. **I will** give them singleness of heart and action, so that they will always fear me for their own good and the good of their children after them. **I will** make an everlasting covenant with them: **I will** never stop doing good to them, and **I will** inspire them to fear me, so that they will never turn away from me. **I will** rejoice in doing them good and will assuredly plant them in this land with all my heart and soul."* Jeremiah 32:38-41

*"Moreover, **I will** give you a new heart and put a new spirit within you; and **I will** remove the heart of stone from your flesh and give you a heart of flesh. **I will** put My Spirit within you and cause you to walk in My statutes, and you will be careful to observe My ordinances...."* Ezekiel 36:26-28

*"And **I will** give them one heart, and put a new spirit within them. And **I will** take the heart of stone out of their flesh and give them a heart of flesh, that they may walk in My statutes and keep My ordinances and do them. Then they will be My people, and **I shall** be their God. But as for those whose hearts go after their detestable things and abominations, **I will** bring their conduct down on their heads," declares the Lord GOD."* Ezekiel 11:19-21

How many "I wills" are there between the Jeremiah and Ezekiel scriptures? [5]

---

[5] Answer: 15 – 'I wills' and 1- 'I shall'

Go back and underline them.

Please reread the above scriptures above asking yourself these two questions:

1. Who will do the work?

2. How long is an everlasting covenant good for?[6]

God loves us so much that He provided the Holy Spirit, the new heart and the love we will need to live the way He wants us to. He promises us again that He will be the one who will inspire us to fear Him. He will give us singleness of heart. He will direct our steps, our hearts, and our lives if we will let Him. He does this so that He will get the glory, not mankind, not me or you.

How does God do this?[7]

Back in chapter 1, Jesus was asking Peter "do you love me" *agape* and Peter answered back "Lord you know I love you" *phileo* love. We find it easy to *phileo* love people but *agape* love is something that is supernatural. You only find it in God, we cannot "drum" it up. *Agape* love is not inside of us unless it has been placed inside us by the source, namely God.

If we have the Holy Spirit a true treasure and jewel, dwelling in our hearts, why then do we not live a totally sinless and carefree life?

---

[6] Answer: 1. God 2. For Ever
[7] Answer: through His Holy Spirit

Why are we so bogged down with life?

Why is life so hard?

Why do we not love the way God talks about?

Thoughts:

I know that often I struggle with believing that my heart is good and that can spill over making me question if I am good. If God has given me a new heart and all that He does is good, and He talks about me and sees me in wondrous ways as in Chapter 3, why am I still struggling through this life?

There can be a few reasons:

- Filters
- Brokenness or blocked areas
- Not realizing whose I am – aligning myself with who God says I am

We have been talking about filters and those filters have been caused by many different things. Some of those filters have been caused by wounds or hurts we have experienced. We have all been wounded in life, we are not "whole hearted". We have broken places or blocked off places in our hearts because the wounds are/were too painful, so we shut off. Some people call these areas strongholds, they can be the places we run to when we are hurting. Strongholds are things which cannot be easily torn down or removed, thus the name "stronghold".

Online dictionary definition of stronghold: *a place that has been fortified so as to protect it against attack.*

A stronghold is a fortified, built up, solid structure, it is not going any place soon and we tend to cling to them or flee to them. We all have been hurt in life, every one of us, we have a pattern that we go to when we hurt, it is familiar and we have conditioned ourselves to run there, it becomes our life preserver. If we are not running to God with our hurts, wounds, these places separate us from God and from ourselves. We do not want to look at these areas; to open these areas up would be painful, so we would rather not go there. We become hardened, critical, negative, we become like the list we mentioned at the start of this chapter, separated from self. We may not see it but others around us are bound to. If we do not want separation from God or ourselves, these areas need to be looked at and cleaned out.

Teacher Demo: need 2 mini mason jars, mini ¼" Styrofoam balls, 4 mini pebbles, walnut (or rock a similar size to a walnut)

Ask: What if our hearts are already full or perhaps our hearts are broken and in pieces, how does God fit in there?

Have the 2 jars and fill one with those little Styrofoam balls. This jar represents our hearts. The Styrofoam balls represent what is in our hearts: me, husband, children, family, friends, job and now add wounds and areas we have hardened – add the 4 mini pebbles. The pebbles represent some filters, block and wounds. Along comes God and we put Him into the mix. Drop the rock or walnut into the jar. The Styrofoam balls should spill up and over the sides. It looks like He does not fit or have access to our whole heart.

Take jar #2 – put the walnut in first, then add the Styrofoam from jar #1 (all the pieces should fit in).

When we put God in first the rest of our life falls into place in every area.

"The Spirit of the Sovereign LORD is on me, because the LORD has anointed me to proclaim good news to the poor. He has sent me to bind up the brokenhearted, to proclaim freedom for the captives and release from darkness for the prisoners" Isaiah 61:1

Brokenhearted the Hebrew Word is: "leb shabar" ("leb" for "heart," and "shabar" for "broken"). Isaiah used the word "shabar" to describe a bush whose "twigs are dry, they are broken off" (27:11); God is speaking literally here. He says, "Your heart is now in many pieces. I want to heal it."[8]

Your heart can be broken. It does not have to be something "big" to cause us to have a broken or wounded heart. We try to fix ourselves and fill those broken areas with what will make us "feel better", otherwise known as imitation pearls. Stop here and think of what some of your "go to's", strongholds are when life hurts or you are stressed: (examples: food, people, alcohol, shopping, sex….)

_____

[8] John Eldredge, *Waking the Dead*, (Nashville, Tennessee: Thomas Nelson, 2003): p. 132)

Our character is shaped by how we deal with or react to what has happened to us; we tend to get better **or** bitter. As the day, days, or even years, go by we either deal with these wounding's or heart issues in an appropriate way with God or we stuff this pain into a box (in our heart), a block.

As we get more and more wounds in this life we have more and more areas that are affected. The result is the cutting off or deadening of places in our hearts, the central place where Gods' Spirit resides. Thus we are not whole-hearted. God has placed a "new" heart into us with the Holy Spirit but we cannot give God our whole heart, because we have blocked a part of it off. We cannot live in the freedom and love God promises if we have blocked areas of our heart. God asks for ALL of us, the whole house, not just pieces of it. We expect God to give us ALL of Himself, and He expects the same in return.

"Jesus replied: 'Love the Lord your God with all your heart and with all your soul and with all your mind.'" Matthew 22:37

When you are not whole hearted, you have a separation from you, yourself **and** God.

A house divided: *"Every kingdom divided against itself will be ruined, and every city or household divided against itself will not stand."* Matthew 12:25

We use many things to try to fix our broken places (passions, isolation – don't talk about it; obsessions – can't stop talking about it). These can be used to fill the broken places and can eventually lead to addictions because we have this constant need to fill those hurting places with "something" besides the pain.

Name some things that could cause our hearts to be broken:

We may not even know there is a blocked off area in our heart but that does not diminish the fact there that is something blocking us and our path to God. These little blocks in the diagram represent heart hurts.

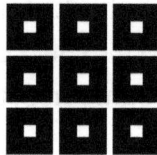

When this blocked-off area or wound is not healed and we chose not to look at it, we can then build a brick wall in front of it (represented by the line underneath the blocks) and pretend it is not there; this is called *denial.*

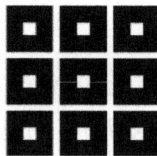

Each time we refuse to look at these areas we build more brick walls in front and eventually it becomes a fortified place that no one is getting into (including ourselves or God).

Separation from God and our self.

Where did the very first separation from God happen?

At the very beginning -

"So the Lord God banished him from the Garden of Eden to work the ground from which he had been taken. After he drove the man out, he placed on the east side of the Garden of Eden cherubim and a flaming sword flashing back and forth to guard the way to the tree of life." Genesis 3:23-24

The first separation began right smack at the beginning of Gods story. Gods' first set of people on the earth, Adam and Eve. If they could not get it right from the start, what hope is there for us?

The biggest source of keeping us separate from God is "us" otherwise known as "me".

"I/Me" and "Fear" get in the way. **I** think **I** know better, **I** think **I** got this; or my pride tells me that **I** am doing okay and **I** do not need anyone else. My pride tells me **I** certainly do not need .... "them." Pride also holds onto "it's not fair" or "do you know what they did to me?" Fear causes paralysis, where we do nothing or it can cause us to run the other way. Adam and Eve picked their own path; they derailed their world right there in the garden and created the first block or separation from God and from themselves.

We get to pick our own path, while we might not have been able to pick our childhood or our filters, we can as adults, can change the path we are on. We can continue to house those blocks and walls in our hearts or we can blow them up, heal them, and allow God to have total access to our hearts and lives.

Adam and Eve's sin affected them, and then it affected all of mankind.

The first man Adam brought sin into this world and it came to stay by tainting the bloodline of all of Adam's children, grandchildren, great-grandchildren and so on, right on down the human line...to us.

Everything we do as people has a consequence whether for good or not. If we refuse to look at these blocks and walls in our hearts and not have the courage to tear them down, this pattern (s) will continue down *our family lines* as well.

Is this the legacy you want to leave behind for your children and grandchildren? Thoughts:

Jesus was the restorer of the break between God and man. Jesus took our sin, not just a part, but all of it upon Himself when He hung on the cross. Enabling all who acknowledge Jesus Christ as their Lord and Savior the opportunity to get restored to God, to close the gap or break that was created by the first Adam.

But what do we do with the blocks that are already in our hearts? God already thought of that too....

"He heals the brokenhearted and binds up their wounds."
Psalm 147:3

"For this people's heart has become calloused; they hardly hear with their ears, and they have closed their eyes. Otherwise they might see with their eyes, hear with their ears, understand with

their hearts and turn, and I would heal them." Matthew 13:15

"The LORD is my shepherd, I lack nothing. He makes me lie down in green pastures, he leads me beside quiet waters, he refreshes my soul. He guides me along the right paths for his name's sake." Psalm 23:1-3

"Heal me, LORD, and I will be healed; save me and I will be saved, for you are the one I praise." Jeremiah 17:14

God promises to not only give us forgiveness of sins but to also "heal" our hearts! Ask Him.

End Song: *Holy Spirit You Are Welcome Here* – Kim Walker Smith

Prayer: Reflect on and ask the Holy Spirit to show you where you have blocks, wounds or separation from yourself and/or God. Ask God to keep you teachable and open to His leading and guiding.

Drawings, Doodles & Notes:

Drawings, Doodles & Notes:

Session 5: Separation from Others

Recap

Sessions 1 Imitation Versus Real Love – Love Circle

Session 2 Separation From God – Who's Your Daddy? Daddy Job Description

Session 3 Who You Are to God – He Knows Your Name

Session 4 Separation from Self – Brokenness/Blocks in our heart

❖

What does it mean to be separated from others?

Separation in any form means "apart". Separation in this sense means that we are cut off, blocked or even broken in our relationships with other people.

Recovery groups, counsellors are always asking us to go back to the past. We get tired of going back there, we feel we have forgiven, forgotten and it is dealt with. But if you have not had that wounded area healed by the ultimate healer – God, it is still there. You are dragging your past around with you and you may not even be aware of it. This is separation from Self.

We are so out of tune with ourselves we cannot see these areas. If we have blocked off areas from God, He cannot get through to us to tell us that this block is there. We cannot hear Him, this is separation from God.

FEAR tries to stop us from going back to the original source of our blocks or wounds. **PAIN** also stops us from going there. We do not want to go back and feel that "stuff" again, its uncomfortable, it hurts and we just do not like it. " **I/me**" get in the way. We tell ourselves we have dealt with it, it is not important or that we do not remember.

God talks about the "heart" 725 times in the Bible – it is a very important subject.

Your heart is the residing place of the Holy Spirit of God. In the Jewish temple in the Old Testament, God resided in the Holy of Holies. In the New Testament it now says He resides inside you – where is <u>your</u> Holy of Holies?[9]

"Do you not know that your yourselves are God's temple, and that God's Spirit dwells in you?" 1 Corinthians 3:16

God is asking: Will you let Me heal you?

Will you let me make you whole hearted?

Can I have the whole house?

I want to give you true pearls – not plastic.

Tell Him: I want my whole heart back!

In order to give you your whole heart back, God will need to do a heart transplant He does not want to give you a bandaid fix. In the physical world, if we have a heart attack or stroke, we know automatically that there is going to be some kind of medical intervention. An angioplasty, angiogram, heart surgery, put in a stint, these are the normal process for a physically ill heart. None of them is pain free.

Why would we be surprised to know that in the spiritual realm we will need to undergo a heart transplant and surgery to get a new and improved, non-plastic heart? It will not be pain free.

When we tell ourselves that we are fine the way we are, we are

---

[9] Answer: your heart

actually saying that we are fine with plastic pearls.

Bottom line: We either deal with our wounds and hurts with God or we will stuff the pain into a box (in our heart). As we get more and more "hurts" we have more and more areas that are affected. These are frozen pain areas. The result is the cutting off or deadening of our hearts. The central place where God resides and where we can access His love.

Your wounds can be caused by many things, but more often than not they will be caused by other people. This leads us to Separation from others.

Separation from others leads to distrust, broken relationships, strained relationships, isolation, paranoia, loneliness, lone ranger complex – I can do it myself, I do not need anyone. God created us to be in relationship with Him, ourselves and others.

People hurt people. Ask anyone if they have ever had another person hurt them and the answer will be a huge resounding YES. From childhood on someone along our way of life has hurt us. The question becomes have you totally healed from it? If you have blocked off areas, or you find you run to unhealthy habits (strongholds), chances are you still have some work to do.

In order to heal you God will take you mentally back to the original "hurt" or "incident." For example, for someone with alcoholic tendencies, alcohol is really not the main problem. The main problem may be that they feel unloved, and everything they have done is to try to find love and the alcohol just numbs the original pain. The root issue is the feeling of being "unlovable." God wants to deal with the "unlovable" feeling, not the alcohol. He is dealing with the identity issue – feeling "unloveable", not the behavior.

Someone with a "rejection" wound may keep pushing other people away with their attitude, words or actions. They could often be described as "prickly". They believe the lie deep inside of them that says they are not worth loving, someone proved it to them long ago by rejecting or hurting them and they have lived their life proving it to be true. The true root is the "not worth loving", they think they are not valuable, self-worth is nonexistent. God wants to heal that part of them, not focus on the behavior. People focus and make judgements on the behavior, on the "what they did" not seeing others as "broken people much like themselves."

If we have ever made a vow, whether inside our mind or with our mouth, we have made a stronghold. Finish this sentence for yourself:
I will never…………………

I will never trust my parents, my siblings, my teacher, my boss, my friend, my daughter, my church, God. I will never shop at that place again. What is your "I will never….."

Whatever you finished that sentence off with is a vow, a fortified place that you have staked territory on and no one is going to get past it. It is an inner promise to yourself and it can only lead to Separation.

For me: for many years, I would never trust a man. I had been hurt by all of the important ones in my life so I convinced myself that all men were not trustworthy.

God has a sense of humor by only giving me boys as my children. I also was the mom who had their male friends around, often my whole world was being surrounded by "guys". I came to see and appreciate the value of men, I now appreciate a man's perspective, logic and knowledge. God and I had to work it out, it took a while and it was not comfortable for me but that vow is now broken. That frozen area in my heart that I struggled to protect with my vow is gone.

Sometimes in our brokenness, we think that God has left us alone so we isolate and do not want to trust other people because they hurt us. The walls in our hearts make us unapproachable. We become cranky and bitter because we have hardened and broken areas.

Disease is another really important reason for us to deal with our wounds and blocks as unresolved wounds can settle inside your body.

"Your boasting is not good. Do you not know that a little yeast leavens the whole batch of dough? Get rid of the old yeast, that you may be a new unleavened batch, as you really are. For Christ, our Passover lamb, has been sacrificed...." 1 Corinthians 5:6-7

Just like the yeast that affects the whole batch of dough, a little unforgiveness, a little hurt, can work in your whole body.

Read the following scriptures:

"Reproach has broken my heart and I am so sick." Psalm 69:20

"A heart at peace gives life to the body, but envy rots the bones."
Proverbs 14:30

Did you ever think that the things *you think* affect your physical body? They do.

"Jesus knew their thoughts and said to them, "Every kingdom divided against itself will be ruined, and every city or household divided against itself will not stand." Matthew 12:25

A house divided is a place of unrest, not safe, not secure. Your body not at rest by brokenness is a place of unrest. Break the word disease down into "dis" and "ease" – the body broken is a place of dis-ease.

I know I personally have had things show up in my physical body that were in direct correlation to my emotional health. To be honest, there are times where I do NOT want to do forgiving, I plain do not want to. I realize that forgiving feels like I am loosing, it feels like my rights are being violated. I can only identify with this because I have been there. I am one who has camped on unforgiveness far too long and seen physical things pop up in my body. My neck or stomach often rebel at being turned into knots at the thought of giving up 'my' rights. I totally get it!

But God wants ALL of us and we know we definitely want ALL of God.

Unforgiveness and Forgiveness each have 3 levels:
God, Self and Others

Funny how this works, 3 levels of separation and 3 levels of forgiveness.

When we go through the healing process for each wound that God brings to mind, we need to ensure we have forgiven on all 3 of these levels. Often we only forgive on 1 level.

Example: My friend betrays a confidence of mine.

i) I can choose to forgive my friend and the incident is done, to be remembered no more

ii) I chose to forgive my friend but I do not let it go and over the next few years I mention it whenever there is a disagreement.

To forgive in the second way means that the incident is not over – I still have business to conduct on forgiveness over this incident.

Next: I take the time to examine this incident with God, it turns out that I am mad at God for not stopping my friend from spreading the information around. Or perhaps I am angry with God for even sending me that "friend". Our healing on this level is asking myself what anger do I hold God accountable for in this incident? It may be none but we still need to look at it to ensure we do not have a block here.

The last level is usually the hardest to forgive – myself. Why did I trust that friend? Why did I tell my friend that information? I "always" wreck things, I "always" say things I should not… and the list of self-condemnation begins to grow.

Anytime you say, "I always…" that is another form of a vow, a forfeited place, a stronghold.

We can even begin to call our self names: "that was so stupid" or "how could I have been so dumb?" This kind of "self-talk" can be a stronghold, we run to this place in our head because we have been conditioned to do so. We can be so amazing at beating ourselves up mentally and when we make vows, it only becomes stronger.

I know for myself, I used to come to God with an attitude of "well God it's me again and yes I blew it, again, I can't believe I did it again......" God never sees us like this. Jesus died for our sins – period. All sins. When God looks at you He sees you sinless – Jesus took them all, they belong to Him.

God never sees us as "again". Only in our own minds are we "blowing it" again and again. Yet we are so quick to believe we are a failure, God never sees you like that. That is why you have to know who God is, who your Daddy is, how He sees you, how He talks about you because that is the only reality that matters.

God, our Dad promises to His children, that for each incident that we ask for forgiveness for:

"For as high as the heavens are above the earth, So great is His lovingkindness toward those who fear Him. As far as the east is from the west, so far has He removed our transgressions from us. Just as a father has compassion on his children, So the LORD has compassion on those who fear Him...."   Psalm 103:11-13

Our Dad promises to forgive us and then remember it no more. If God can forgive and remember it no more, why do we replay the tapes in our mind over and over instead of pushing them as far as the east and the west? To not heal and forgive on all 3 levels will result in a blocked off areas, a hardened area in our heart.

Do we need to deal with every little thing – because we all have stuff ?

NO—only if the incident results in negative behavior. We also do not have to make things up; God is quite able to direct us where we need to go in our healing.

End Song: *Trust in You, Lauren Daigle*

Prayer: Take some time and ask the Holy Spirit to begin to give you a list of things in your heart that are blocking you from God, Yourself and Others. As memories or thoughts come up, write them down, make sure you have forgiven each incident on all 3 levels – God, Yourself, Others. Work through the list with God one item at a time.

Drawings, Doodles & Notes:

Drawings, Doodles & Notes:

Session 6: Are You Jesus?

Opening Song: *What if Jesus Came Back Like That?* Colin Raye

Read: The Apple Cart Story (author unknown)

A few years ago, a group of salesmen went to a regional sales convention in Chicago. The convention lasted all week, and all the salesmen had assured their wives that they would be home in plenty of time for Friday night's dinner.

As they hurried to the airport to catch their return flight, they rushed down the airport's corridor with their briefcases in hand. In their rush, one of these salesmen inadvertently kicked over a cart which held a display of apples.

Apples flew everywhere. Without stopping or looking back, they all continued running so they would make their plane.

All but one.

He stopped after running a few more yards, took a deep breath, and experienced a twinge of compassion for the girl whose apple stand had been overturned.

He told his buddies to go on without him, waved goodbye, told one of them to call his wife when they arrived home and explain why he was taking a later flight. Then he returned to the cart where the apples were all over the terminal floor.

He was glad he did.

The 16-year-old girl running the apple cart was totally blind. She was softly crying, tears running down her cheeks in frustration, and at the same time helplessly groping for her spilled produce as

the crowd swirled about her, no one stopping and no one to care for her plight.

The salesman knelt on the floor with her, gathered up the apples, put them back on the cart and helped organize her display.

As he did this, he noticed that many of the apples had become battered and bruised; these he set aside in another basket.

When he had finished, he pulled out his wallet and said to the girl, "Here, please take this $40 for the damage we did. Are you okay?"

She nodded through her tears.

He continued on with, "I hope we didn't spoil your day too badly."

As the salesman started to walk away, the bewildered blind girl called out to him, "Mister....."
He paused and turned to look back into her blind eyes.

She continued, "Are you Jesus?"

❖

"Are you Jesus?"

Do others see the resemblance of Jesus in you?

Do you see a resemblance of Jesus in yourself?

Tough questions but necessary if we want to have a family resemblance to our heavenly Father.

When we use the resource of the Holy Spirit that lives inside us, this precious gift given to us, we allow God to use His temple or "our body" to love others.   Then, '***we do become***' Jesus to other people.   ***We are*** His hands and feet, ***we are*** His love to be spread throughout our world.

Remember the two things that will block you in getting your heart free – *Fear and I/Me.*

Will you let Him use you?

Will you let God love through you so that others will see Jesus in you?

"I lay down my life for my sheep" John 10:15, 18

"Greater love has no one than this, that he lay down his life..." John 15:12,13

"A new command I give you: Love one another. As I have loved you, so you must love one another. By this everyone will know that you are my disciples, if you love one another." John 13:34-35

"This is how we know what love is: Jesus Christ laid down his life for us. And we ought to lay down our lives for our brothers and sisters." 1 John 3:16

Love is a *command*, but how do we actually do it? Write your thoughts here:

Light Bulb Thought: If our purpose is to the cause of humanity, where we think we are placed here to "serve" others, we most likely will be defeated and brokenhearted. Often the people *we think* we are to "serve" are ungrateful and we quickly get deflated and discouraged. If our motivation is to serve God, and we work only to serve Him, it will not matter what other people say or do.

You might need to read that last paragraph a couple of times over and go slowly so it will absorb right into your soul.

Paul persecuted and killed Christians and yet God still loved him enough to save him. Now as a follower and servant of God, Paul went on to have a list of things other people had done to him:

"Are they servants of Christ?—I speak as if insane—I more so; in far more labors, in far more imprisonments, beaten times without number, often in danger of death. Five times I received from the Jews thirty-nine lashes. Three times I was beaten with rods, once I was stoned, three times I was shipwrecked, a night and a day I have spent in the deep. I have been on frequent journeys, in dangers from rivers, dangers from robbers, dangers from my countrymen, dangers from the Gentiles, dangers in the city, dangers in the wilderness, dangers on the sea, dangers among false brethren; I have been in labor and hardship, through many sleepless nights, in hunger and thirst, often without food, in cold and exposure. Apart from such external things, there is the daily pressure on me of concern for all the churches..." 2 Corinthians 11:23-28

Why do you think Paul continued to follow God after all these incidents?

Would you continue to follow God if all these things had happened to you? Why or why not?

"That is why, for the sake of Christ, I delight in weaknesses, insults, in hardships, in persecutions, in difficulties. For when I am weak, then I am strong." 2 Corinthians 12:10

<u>*"For the sake of Christ"*</u> Please go back and underline this phrase in the 2 Corinthians 12:10 scripture. Paul's love for Jesus overruled all human emotions. My devotion must be to God, not to people and the byproduct of my life is a heart that loves others with Gods love. Notice that love is a byproduct not the action itself, the action is to love God.

Our brokenness, wounding or strongholds keep us separated from others. God has asked us to love our neighbors as ourselves. He has even provided the Love from Himself through the Holy Spirit. If we have blocks and separations we cannot feel Gods love, and we cannot love ourselves, how then can we possibly love others? Thoughts:

Some people are easy to love, our hearts love to be with them, they make us happy. But do we love them with human love- *phileo* or   God love - *agape ?*   <u>Circle One</u>

Is our love conditional?   Example: I love that person until they hurt me, bug me, lie to me, betray me…

Can you name someone that you love unconditionally? That is, no matter what they did to you or to someone else you would still love them. Write the names here:

But is that what God actually said?

"Love the Lord your God with ALL your heart soul and mind and love your neighbors as yourself." Luke 10:27

Neighbors – hmmmm. Who are our neighbors…

For the best definition, we should read the Good Samaritan Story in Luke 10:25-37:

"On one occasion an expert in the law stood up to test Jesus. "Teacher," he asked, "what must I do to inherit eternal life?"

"What is written in the Law?" he replied. "How do you read it?"

He answered, "'Love the Lord your God with all your heart and with all your soul and with all your strength and with all your mind'; and, 'Love your neighbor as yourself.'"

"You have answered correctly," Jesus replied. "Do this and you will live."

But he wanted to justify himself, so he asked Jesus, "And who is my neighbor?"

In reply Jesus said: "A man was going down from Jerusalem to Jericho, when he was attacked by robbers. They stripped him of his clothes, beat him and went away, leaving him half dead. A priest happened to be going down the same road, and when he saw the man, he passed by on the other side. So too, a Levite, when he came to the place and saw him, passed by on the other side. But a Samaritan, as he traveled, came where the man was; and when he saw him, he took pity on him. He went to him and bandaged his wounds, pouring on oil and wine. Then he put the man on his own donkey, brought him to an inn and took care of him. The next day he took out two denarii and gave them to the innkeeper. 'Look after him,' he said, 'and when I return, I will reimburse you for any extra expense you may have.'

"Which of these three do you think was a neighbor to the man who fell into the hands of robbers?"

The expert in the law replied, "The one who had mercy on him."

Jesus told him, "Go and do likewise."

This story is between 2 men, 2 opposing people groups, 2 different cultures, 2 different teachings, different everything. Their "families", "friends" or "church" would not agree with how this story played out. Samaritans were a mixed blood race, resulting from intermarriage of Israel and Gentiles, something that was never supposed to happen. John 4:9 calls these people "unclean". A better term might be "untouchables." You did not associate with "those" people, you avoided them at all costs. Yet the Good Samaritan, the untouchable, the half breed, the "enemy" had pity and compassion on his "enemy".

He had compassion when others walked right by on the other side of the road. "Those others", would have been the ones that the victim thought was his friends, his fellow worshipers. They were "his people" but they walked by on the other side of the road, avoiding him.

Who are 'your' enemies?

Who are your "half breeds?" Who would you walk by on the other side or cross the road to avoid?

Did you come up with terms like: Prostitutes, beggars, sales people, Islam, Muslims, JW's, drunk or high people, bikers....

If we think we do not have prejudices, think again, we all do and they come from our filters, usually from our families of origin. God hates prejudices, He has none.

God did not give us the Good Samaritan story as a nice story, but rather as an illustration of how to love. It cost the Samaritan something, it cost his pride to look upon his enemy with compassion, it took physical work to bring the hurt man to the inn, it took sacrifice, it took his time, it took his money to ensure the beaten man would be well cared for. It cost the Samaritan to care for the injured man.

The Good Samaritan is a direct arrow pointing us to Jesus both as the Samaritan and the beaten man. Jesus crossed the road for us; He crossed from heaven to earth to bring salvation to a world that would not accept Him. While He was on earth He reached out in compassion to hurting, injured and troubled people. People who could not pay Him back. It took physical work to heal them, it took a sacrifice of time and commitment. Jesus was rarely left alone. It cost Jesus to care for the injured and hurting. Many of them hated Him, and they beat Him and ended up killing Him. His battered, tortured body was placed in a tomb and He was left for dead. His friends, the disciples, ran away, He was left alone. His death bore the penalty for our sins, He took our punishment. Jesus was the role model on how to love.

God has asked us to love people – ALL people. He has given us the tools to love them. If we have the Holy Spirit then we have access to the whole Love circle, all 16 segments. We have all those same 16 segments inside of us, think about it.

Why is it we find some people are just too hard to love?[10]

It could be 'Fear' because we may not want that person in our life for various reasons: they drag us down emotionally, they are needy, they are always asking for something from us, I really do not like them; I am afraid of what it will cost me.

The other reason is 'I' - because pride and selfishness take over.

---

[10] Answer: "Fear and I" get in the way

Who are these people who just seem too hard to love? People you have not talked to in years? People you have not forgiven? People who hurt you? People who hurt your family?

Prayerfully write a list here of the people who just seem too hard to love:

If you still feel that pang of hurt when you are thinking of that person then those hurts are still wounding you. You are keeping the incidents and words that originally affected you inside your body, letting them fester and continue to harm you to this day. That other person is still harming you years later because you did not take these wounds to the Cross. These are the people who you crossed the road to avoid.

I do not say this lightly, or that it is even easy; this is hard work, but it is work that has to be done for anyone wanting to live in the freedom that Jesus died to give you.

God commands us to forgive, not because He wants us to forget the incidents or to let someone off the hook. He commands us to forgive because He first forgave you.

He knows **_you_** cannot heal without forgiveness. Did you get that? YOU, cannot heal without it.

Who do you need to forgive?

We as humans have a hard time with the fact that God wants you to trust Him with any and all revenge and retaliation. God loves _you_ too much to let _you_ keep harming yourself this way in unforgiveness. God is offering you a real pearl – 'freedom', that is what freedom is, but too often we cling to the imitation.

**Please hear this: You do not harm the other person by not forgiving them, you only harm yourself. If something someone said or did still makes you mad or hurt, weeks, months, or even years down the road - they are still hurting you.

Litmus test: when you think of that person or the "incident" do you still feel a pang in your gut. If yes, they are still affecting you. It is time to get off of the hook they have you stuck on and free yourself from this event. Regardless if the other person asks for forgiveness or never does, you need to do this for yourself.

By forgiving you are not forgetting, that is not what God has asked of you. It would not be smart to forget that someone tried to hurt you and give them your trust back. It would not be smart to forget that someone stole from you and then you trust them with your money.

But it would be really not smart for you to hang on to the pain and hurt that you are inflicting on yourself by not forgiving.

It has nothing to do with who deserves what; it has everything to do with your healing and your relationship with God, healing your heart.

Read that last paragraph again please. Perhaps read it as many times as it takes for the meaning to sink in.

Forgiveness has nothing to do with who deserves what. God demands to be the retaliator in all situations and He expects us to trust Him. He also commands us to forgive, not because He does not care, but exactly the opposite, because He knows it is for our own good, in body, mind, and spirit. True freedom = real treasure.

God wants to heal these areas, these locked-off, hurt and broken areas.

Many of us today are stunted in our emotional and spiritual walk because we shut off our emotions and heart at the age or moment when some kind of hurt or trauma was directed to us.

God wants our hearts to be free from the boxes, blocks and brokenness. He will not remove them for us, He will **always, always** ask for permission. Trust Him, He is faithful to help you through the pain.

It might not be easy, and if you were severely abused, I would strongly suggest to you that you should walk through this step with a counsellor who can help guide you through it.

The fact of it is, **all of us** are broken, **we all** have areas in our lives that have been hurt and damaged; areas that are still blocked off to God, ourselves, and others.

Please Note: If you are a prayer warrior and you want to help people in their healing, it is important to realize this cycle of hurts and traumas. If you are praying for healing for someone for a physical ailment, and you do not pray for healing of the heart, and that ailment is a symptom or result of some internal wounding you are only putting a bandaid on the problem.

The Holy Spirit wants all of the house, your whole heart, not just a few select pieces. Perhaps it is time to clean house!

Remember that your Daddy, the Daddy of Perfect Love and the One Who is the Complete Daddy Job Description is going to go there with you. You can trust Him.

End Song: *The Hurt and The Healer*, Mercy Me

Prayer: Take some time and ask God to show you where you are broken, blocked, stuffed, or had damage done to your heart. This is not a quick or pain-free question to ask God, because the damage done in pain to your heart can only be healed or accessed through the same pain.   This step is ESSENTIAL to living in the freedom that God wants for you.

A good litmus test question: I love everybody except...............

Go through the list *forgiving on all 3 levels.*
Start to pray for those who hurt you, it will not be easy at first, but ask God to show you how He sees them. Tell Him you do not know how to love them, ask Him to give you His love for them, and that you will *be willing* to feel love towards them. (notice it does not say you have to go to them, talk to them or confront them, but to start to be *willing to feel,* these are the first steps in unblocking).

Drawings, Doodles & Notes:

Drawings, Doodles & Notes:

Session 7: Loving Others

Recap

Session 5 Are you Jesus? The Apple Cart Story, Do people see the family resemblance of Jesus in you? Love is a command yet who do we cross the street to avoid? Forgiveness is not about who deserves what, it is for our own good.

Session 6 I will love everyone except....

❖

Opening Song: Show Me My Heart Lord by Casting Crowns

When I was listening to this song before God downloaded this content to me, I started to weep. You see God was taking me through some excruciating pain as I write this. The teacher always has to learn the lesson first. My heart is breaking, hurting at the pain that is threatening it. My eyes are red and swollen, Kleenex lays in piles on the floor. I have in anguish poured out my heart to God telling Him that this hurts, knowing Gods' expectation of me is to love in spite of the pain. I told Him I did not know how – it is not evenly humanly possible.

I was going along knowing that God could and would love through me but I <u>was ignoring the fact that it costs something of me to allow that.</u> I was thinking I did not have the right to acknowledge the pain of my heart break while loving others, especially if I was called to love the unlovable.

<u>I was not loving myself</u>. I thought that being called to love the unloveable meant that I had to ignore "my pain." But that is not what God is asking, when He says – "Love your neighbor as yourself" – the two go hand in hand. You cannot do one without the other.

Let me explain: I realized that God knew that the pain was there all along and He wanted access to it; to allow me to be honest and to allow Him to heal the hurt. I cried and cried and told Him all the things that were unfair and all the things that I did not like about this heartbreak and how much pain it cost me. I told Him I was hurting, but He already knew that.

Two days earlier God had restored me to a wonderful place of intimacy with Him, it was delightful and then, then, He started to deal with my pain. As I was crying and trying to figure Him out, I asked Him about the sequence, why I could not heal first. Why could the pain not come first and then He could leave me with the joyous intimacy? I wanted to go on feeling the delightful good stuff rather than saving the "icky" stuff for last.

He told me that you cannot "grieve" or "give your hurt to Him" (or anyone) unless you trust Him first. I had to be in a place of intimacy before I would allow myself to trust Him with my pain. We need to be so close to God, to have no barriers, and no filters so we can trust Him with our pain.

This is why it is so vitally important that we believe in the Love Circle and the Daddy of the Daddy Job Description; it is a trust and healing issue.

You may be having a hard time believing all of the segments, especially if you have been hurt or have ever wondered, "God where are you?" Or "God where were you?"

King David asked the same questions, over and over in the psalms. The Psalms are meant for the brokenhearted. They ask the same questions you and I ask, but David always comes back to: "God I trust you", even when he could not humanly see it. It is not wrong to ask the questions, it is not wrong to have the pain, it is not wrong to wonder why, God can handle those questions,

He can take your anger and your questions. You may get an answer but you might not, that is a God choice.

In the end it comes down to your choice: you believe God is trustworthy or you do not. You will either trust Him with your pain and hurt or you will not. It is a matter of your will.

I was there: I did not want to forgive and could not understand the hurt and then God softly spoke to me about who I was before He saved me. How disrespectfully I treated Him and I start to get a sense of "wow" over my own behavior. Sometimes He asks me if I would like it if He did not forgive me of "**my**" sins? That one always hits home, of course not. I always want God to forgive me. It is then that I realize that I have no rights whatsoever, because apart from the grace of God, I would be just as unloveable and just as miserable to live with. I know; I am still working at it.

Who am I to charge God with unfair, when He did everything for me? He loved me before I was saved, He loved you before you were saved. He loved you at your very worst.

How much does love cost?   Thoughts on this:

Did you ever stop to think that love cost you anything? Is this a new thought?

Did you still think of love as just an emotion: warm and fuzzy?

Love *is not* a noun word: a person, place or thing or an adjective – a description word. Love *is a verb*: an action word.

Action words require something from us – **action**. If love cost God "Everything" by the death of His Son, then why do we think it would be wrong or unfair to have it cost us something?

Love costs… Everything!

Love… Hurts!

" *Are they servants of Christ? (I am out of my mind to talk like this.) I am more. I have worked much harder, been in prison more frequently, been flogged more severely, and been exposed to death again and again. Five times I received from the Jews the forty lashes minus one. Three times I was beaten with rods, once I was pelted with stones, three times I was shipwrecked, I spent a night and a day in the open sea, I have been constantly on the move. I have been in danger from rivers, in danger from bandits, in danger from my fellow Jews, in danger from Gentiles; in danger in the city, in danger in the country, in danger at sea; and in danger from false believers. I have labored and toiled and have often gone without sleep; I have known hunger and thirst and have often gone without food; I have been cold and naked…"*
2 Corinthians 11:23-28   Paul was an experiment in hurt.

Luke 9:7-9   John the Baptist was beheaded

11 of the 12 disciples were martyred.

Jonah was told to go to the Ninevites, the enemy.

Love costs and it hurts – it requires something of us.

"Then the word of the LORD came to Jonah a second time: "Go to the great city of Nineveh and proclaim to it the message I give you." Jonah 3:1-2

Joseph, sold by his brothers, forced into slavery by his very family, then onto jail - it hurt. Genesis 37

Daniel, loved God but his commitment cost him, he was a slave. Daniel 1

Love Costs and Love Hurts

God Himself loved us so much that He gave His one and only Son to die in your place. John 3:16

It Hurt.

How much does love cost? Biblically love costs - Everything.

How much does love hurt? Biblically love is - Excruciating.

God knows how much love costs and He knows how much love costs you. He has not asked something of us that He has not already provided a solution for. It is His love working through us, not ours.

My love has restrictions, complications, filters, strings attached and His love has none.

Oswald Chambers says:

"The fountains from which love flows are in God, not in us. It is absurd to think that the love of God is naturally in our hearts, as a result of our own nature. His love is there only because it 'has been poured out in our hearts by the Holy Spirit.' Romans 5:5 If we try to prove how much we love Him, it is a sure sign that we really do not love Him. The evidence of our love for Him is the absolute spontaneity of our love, which flows naturally from His nature within us. The life of God exhibits itself in this spontaneous way because the fountains of His love are in the Holy Spirit." [11]

The term "**_Yabutt_**" comes to mind here, a very Hebrew sounding word.

"*Yabutt*" translation: "ya, but you don't know what they did" Or "ya, but it is not fair" Or "ya, but I don't want to."

When God says love your enemies, this is a commandment not a suggestion. You see God already has loved your enemies.

Did you get that? God already has loved your enemies. God already provided the solution.

God has already loved your enemies, those people who hurt you, abused you, treated you in such a hateful way – He loved them. God sent His Son to be the Savior of the world, not just your world – *"the"* world.

When did God love you? Was it before or after you were saved?

That is correct – before. You did not have to do anything for God to love you. You did not have to be good enough, you did not have to act a certain way, you did not have to even love Him back. He plain LOVED you before you even knew Him. He loves your enemies the same.

What if you are sleeping with the enemy? Oh my, that gets personal does it not? Our husband, or our wives. He has already provided the solution. **His Love**

What if your enemy has hurt you or your children? He has already provided the solution. **His love.**

---

[11] *My Upmost for His Highest*, Oswald Chambers April 30

Our only requirement **is to get out of the way.** This is truly the hardest of all lessons to learn, and the hardest to do because of the "yabutt's".

God asks us to put down our rights, get over the unfairness, give those things to God to handle and retaliate and allow God to use us for His own purposes. We need to understand that if God loved us and we were "unloveable"; if He did that for us, what right do we have to expect Him to not love others the same? What makes us so darn special but not other people? "I/Me" gets in the way.

When did Jesus die for us?

"While we were yet sinners...." Romans 5:8

"We have no right to decide where we should be placed, or to have preconceived ideas as to what God is preparing us to do. God engineers everything and wherever He places us, our one supreme goal should be to pour out our lives in wholehearted devotion to Him." [12]

"For His Glory". Remember why Paul was willing to face all those hardships; for Christ's sake. It was for Gods Glory because it is not really about us. I/Me wants to believe it is all about me.

God wants all of us, not just pieces or certain rooms of the house, He wants the whole house. God did not give us only pieces of Himself, He gave us His "all" and He expects nothing less in return.

---

[12] *My Upmost for His Highest*, Oswald Chambers, April 23

"As a result, people brought the sick into the streets and laid them on beds and mats so that at least Peter's shadow might fall on some of them as he passed by." Acts 5:15

Peter was so "full" of God that even his shadow healed people as He passed by.

Can you imagine it? So full of God that even your shadow has supernatural power. God had the whole house in Peter's case.

Let me ask you: why do we not like to pray for patience?

Write your answer here:

We know that to attain patience, it takes the trials of life and practice to perfect it. We long to avoid the trials.

So when we pray for God to teach us to "love" how will we learn it?

By trails of life and practice.

So what will God do to teach us to "love"? ...... Practice.

Who will we practice on? .... People

If we examine our lives we will see people in one of two categories: easy to love and not so much.

Guess what God says about each kind of person? "Love them".

God's whole "job description" is about people. God is in the people business and so should we be. There is no person who is so poor off, so smelly, so sick, so dirty, so naked, so evil that they are not in Gods mind and heart to love them.

Who drives you crazy?

Who hurt you?

Who will you not talk to?

Who do you avoid? Who will you cross the street to avoid?

Who will you not forgive?

These unlovable, miserable, smelly, horrible other drivers, obnoxious neighbors, liars, cheaters and stealers are the people God died for. What is worse is that we were in that same group of people! If God laid down His life for them – He has every right to ask you to do the same.

God asks you to lay down your life for your "friend" – remember Jesus called you his "friend."

"Lay down your life for your friend..." John 15:13

"I have called you friends." John 15:15

 In essence He is asking you to lay down, and surrender your life to Him, since He first laid down His life for you. Salvation is easy only because it cost God so much.

Try this:

(Your Name), I want you to lay down your life for (Put persons' name you find to be unlovable in here). I want you to give up your rights for (unlovable person).

Love hurts and love costs. It hurt God immensely and it cost Him everything. Why are we surprised when it hurts and costs us too?

It is interesting that those people we love the most can usually be the ones who hurt us the most – our family, our church, our friends.

Light Bulb Thought: *"Think of it. Your marriage, your family, our Church, your Christian friendships are the greatest and most significant testimony you have"* [13]

Have you ever thought of that? Your marriage, your family, your church, your friends are the most significant testimony you have; if your walk does not match your talk, people will not take what you say seriously. Are you as loving to your family members, your spouse, your kids, as you are to strangers? If you talk God talk, you had better walk the God walk.

Do not for one second think that the world around you is not watching. They are watching "everything". Christians are some of the most scrutinized people in the world and your testimony in reality is your home, your family, your church and your friends.

Examples:

1. Your neighbors hear you shouting and cursing at each other through the open window, yet they know you go to church and preach love and forgiveness. What do you think they think about your "church" and your "God"?

---

[13] *Fragile, Handle with Care,*   Marana Tha

2. You arrive at the school madder than a hornet to ream out your child's teacher because Johnny got yelled at by her today. She knows you go to church, Johnny had mentioned it. What kind of testimony of Love does that say?

What would be a better way to handle this one?

In restaurants is it a well-known fact that servers do not like to wait on the Christians. Apparently we are known to be more picky, more rude and do not tip well. What does your life say to the world?

<u>I hate religion</u>, does that shock you? Truly, I am not a fan. Write your version of Religion here before reading on:

Religion is "rules". Religion never makes a person feel good enough. Religion tries to shame a person into conforming. Religion allows for prejudices and pride. Religion never offers a person freedom. Religion is about right "doing" and always striving. Religion is what the world has been offered by many "churches" for way too long and it is imitation plastic.

I prefer to have relationship. God is about relationship. Relationship is about right "being". God wants a relationship with me and with you. Relationship is the true treasure.

"AND YOU SHALL LOVE THE LORD YOUR GOD WITH ALL YOUR HEART, AND WITH ALL YOUR SOUL, AND WITH ALL YOUR MIND, AND WITH ALL YOUR STRENGTH.' "The second is this, 'YOU SHALL LOVE YOUR NEIGHBOR AS YOURSELF.' There is no other commandment greater than these" Mark 12:30-31

This is the very foundation of relationship: LOVE.

It never was about the rules, it has always been about the Love. That is why Paul endured the hardships thrust upon him, that is why the Apostles could not deny their Jesus after the resurrection, that is why Jesus died on the cross. It is about relationship and that relationship is based on Love.

"The evangelist, Henry Drummond, used a magnet and a piece of steel to illustrate Jesus' command that we love one another as He loved us. He said that if we take a piece of steel and attach it to a

magnet, in time the magnetic properties of the magnet will be acquired by the piece of steel ... and it, too, will be a magnet."[14]

The steel after certain length of time, after hanging out with the magnet becomes magnetized – it takes on the magnets properties. Let us get so close to God that God's love transfers over onto and into us. Let us take on God's properties. Let us be SO full of God that our presence changes things, we will change every atmosphere into which we step, even our shadows will have a positive effect.

"If my people who are called by my name would humble themselves and pray (love) then I will hear from heaven and heal their land." 2 Chronicles 7:14

End Song: *When the God Man Passes By,* Casting Crowns

Prayer: Ask God to show you who in your life, you find "unloveable". Ask God for a supernatural love for that person, ask God to Bless that person. Ask God to show you where you still have "religion" in your life, where you are still striving to live up to the "rules". Ask God to show you what relationship with Him looks like. Tell Him you are open to live in relationship not rules.

---

[14] Henry Drummond, Associate D. L Moody

Drawings, Doodles & Notes:

Drawings, Doodles & Notes:

Session 8: Truth

Recap

Separation from God, Self and Others

Magnet and Steel – let the Love of God transfer over onto and into us, so we can transfer it to others

Last week we looked at loving the unlovable. God is asking us to love other people and not just nice people – persnickety people, unlovable people.

We talked about forgiveness: We said forgiving is not forgetting.

We talked about religion which is imitation versus relationship which is real treasure.

❖

In my NIV Bible in the "notes" section under Romans 5:15 it says: *"death begins with spiritual separation from God and culminates in physical death".*

Interesting to note that "death" begins with separation from God.

Jesus said in John 10:10 *"The thief comes only to steal and kill and destroy; I have come that they may have life, and have it to the full."*

Jesus says He came to give us "Life".

Two distinct opposites and we get to decide which side we wish to align with, death or life.

We have been studying the effect of separation from God, Self and Others.

Today we discuss Truth.

Rick Warren says:

"One of the clearest and best-known statements by Jesus is "I am the way, the truth, and the life. No one can come to the Father except through me" (John 14:6 NLT).

Notice Jesus says, "I am the truth …" He doesn't say truth is a religion or a ritual or a set of rules and regulations. He says "I." Truth is a person.

This is what separates Jesus Christ from every other leader of every other faith. Other leaders have said, "I'm looking for the truth" or "I'm teaching the truth" or "I point to the truth" or "I'm a prophet of truth." Jesus comes and says, "I am the truth."

A lot of people say, "I think Jesus was just a great teacher." But he couldn't be just that. No great teacher would claim to be God if he wasn't. Either Jesus is conning 2.3 billion people who believe a lie, or he was nuts — or Jesus is who he said he was.

Everybody's betting his or her life on something. I'm betting my life that Jesus is who he said he was.

What are you betting your life on?"[15]

In this day and age the word "tolerance" is used, we have to be tolerant of others beliefs and views and we each have our own view of "truth" so what is truth?

Who has truth? Write your comments here:

---

[15] Rick Warren, *Bet Your Life on Jesus*, May 21, 2014 web:
http://pastorrick.com/devotional/english/bet-your-life-on-jesus-christ

One of the segments of our love circle is "truth". God has given us His love and part of His love is Truth – it is who He is. We cannot love without truth. Truth can come easily or it can be hard and uncomfortable. Jesus often said the uncomfortable. We often think we have to be polite and not make waves. Jesus made waves but never at the cost of human dignity.

I think the best the scripture for us to use with truth is:

"Behold, I send you out as sheep in the midst of wolves. Therefore be wise as serpents and harmless as doves." Matthew 10:16

What does it mean to be wise as serpents and harmless as doves? Thoughts on what this would look like?

Being truthful and loving does not take the consequences out of the equation. The reality is that there are consequences for behavior – spiritually and physically. Truth follows the "tough love" disciplinary actions. God does not let us away with our behavior, our Daddy circle says our Daddy disciplines us, we know it and can expect it.

It means that truth needs to be spoken but it needs to be done not by attacking the person but focusing on the behavior. It needs to be done in LOVE.

How did Jesus handle truth? Let us look at The Woman at the Well:

" 'I have no husband'," she replied.

Jesus said to her, "You are right when you say you have no husband. The fact is, you have had five husbands, and the man you now have is not your husband. What you have just said is quite true.'" John 4: 17-18 (whole story 4-46)

Wow Jesus just put it out there for her. But it was not done in a condemning way, He was not belittling her or putting her down. He simply spoke "truth".

We, you and I, might have been tempted to add a few things, little digs here and there attacking her character. "I've noticed that you get around." "Your behavior could be described as trampy," "Did you see what she was wearing, it is no wonder...."

No, God never belittles us in this way. He does not add the digs, the sarcasm.

Look at the woman caught in adultery who they brought to Jesus to have her stoned to death as was the "law" (rules).

"So when they continued asking him, he lifted up himself, and said unto them, 'He that is without sin among you, let him first cast a stone at her." John 8:3-11

Jesus was a rule breaker. According to Jewish law, Jewish rule stated that anyone caught in adultery (male and female, we have to wonder where the man was in this story) was condemned to die by stoning. Jesus broke the law by not condemning this woman, instead He brought the attention back from the woman caught in adultery to the judges. He went from rules to relationship.

He went on to speak truth to the woman but left her dignity intact.

Jesus straightened up and asked her, "Woman, where are they? Has no one condemned you?" "No one, sir," she said. "Then neither do I condemn you," Jesus declared. "Go now and leave your life of sin." John 8:10-11

Cleansing of the Temple

"Now the Passover of the Jews was at hand, and Jesus went up to Jerusalem. And He found in the temple those who sold oxen and sheep and doves, and the money changers doing business. When He had made a whip of cords, He drove them all out of the temple, with the sheep and the oxen, and poured out the changers' money and overturned the tables. And He said to those who sold doves, "Take these things away! Do not make My Father's house a house of merchandise!" John 2:13-16

Do you think there was uncomfortableness associated with these incidents? Do you think Jesus should not have made people feel uncomfortable?

Write your thoughts here:

How do you handle uncomfortableness - with truth or avoidance?

Love is a hard emotion, we have seen and talked about the fact that it takes courage to love completely; *fear and I* get in the way. We are to love God, our Self and Others. The first step is to get out of the way and to let God take over completely.

To lay down our life for our friend; God has asked us to lay down our life for Him just like He laid down His life for you.

Love circle = all of these things are to be lived out in our life but not by our own will power. God has given us ALL of Himself to do this. If we will step out of the way, lay down our rights and let God have 100% of us then it will be possible.

What does the Bible say about truth?

"Behold, You desire truth in the inward parts, And in the hidden part You will make me to know wisdom." Psalm 51:6

"I have not spoken in secret, from somewhere in a land of darkness; I have not said to Jacob's descendants, 'Seek me in vain.' I, the LORD, speak the truth; I declare what is right." Isaiah 45:19

"These are the things you are to do: Speak the truth to each other, and render true and sound judgment in your courts" Zechariah 8:16

"Yet a time is coming and has now come when the true worshipers will worship the Father in the Spirit and in truth, for they are the kind of worshipers the Father seeks." John 4:23

"Then you will know the truth, and the truth will set you free." John 8:32

"But when the Comforter is come, whom I will send unto you from the Father, even the Spirit of truth, which proceedeth from the Father, he shall testify of me." John 15:26

"I am the way the truth and the life." John 14:6

The Bible says that Jesus is Truth, the Holy Spirit is Truth – God is truth. The Bible also says that truth is FREEDOM.

Truth is a Person. Truth is a component of Love. (Love circle graph)

"If I am delayed, you will know how people ought to conduct themselves in God's household, which is the church of the living God, the pillar and foundation of the truth." 1 Timothy 3:15

"The Spirit clearly says that in later times some will abandon the faith and follow deceiving spirits and things taught by demons. Such teachings come through hypocritical liars, whose consciences have been seared as with a hot iron. They forbid people to marry and order them to abstain from certain foods, which God created to be received with thanksgiving by those who believe and who know the truth." 1 Timothy 4:1-3

"Instead, speaking the truth in love, we will grow to become in every respect the mature body of him who is the head, that is, Christ." Ephesians 4:15

Look at 1 Corinthians 13:6

"Love does not delight in evil but rejoices in the Truth."

So when our friend comes up and says, "Do you like my new dress?" What are you going to say?

Oh you thought I was talking about the "big" stuff – the big lies. I mean could these little ones really matter?

Please find me the scripture that says that.

We are talking about Truth. Look again at the circle of Love. It is complete, it is 100%. I cannot take a piece out of it, even a little piece and think it is complete. Love and truth are simultaneous.

I cannot tell a little lie and think that I still have the 100% truth.....

Let us have a look at our Peter story again:

"When they had finished eating, Jesus said to Simon Peter, "Simon son of John, do you love me more than these?"

"Yes, Lord," he said, "you know that I love you."

Jesus said, "Feed my lambs."

Again Jesus said, "Simon son of John, do you love me?"

He answered, "Yes, Lord, you know that I love you."

Jesus said, "Take care of my sheep."

The third time he said to him, "Simon son of John, do you love me?"

Peter was hurt because Jesus asked him the third time, "Do you love me?" He said, "Lord, you know all things; you know that I love you."

Jesus said, "Feed my sheep." John 21:15-17

Peter was hurt but Jesus was calling Peter out into "Truth". God works only in Truth, and so should we. When God uses His Truth in our lives it changes things. It can hurt but it is one of the catalysts God uses to help us grow and learn. Jesus was asking Peter to feed and take care of His sheep.

Who are the sheep? [16]

---

[16] Other People

Those people who can be easy or hard to love, but we are to care for them, instruct them, feed them, guide them and love them.

Peters Shadow

"As a result, people brought the sick into the streets and laid them on beds and mats so that at least Peter's shadow might fall on some of them as he passed by. Crowds gathered also from the towns around Jerusalem, bringing their sick and those tormented by impure spirits, and all of them were healed."   Acts 5:15-16

Hold on! This is the same man but a very different Peter we see here in Acts than the one we saw in Matthew 26:69-75. He ran away in fear for his life the night before the crucifixion, He denounced Jesus to others. Peter had disowned Jesus three times in one evening and now he was so full of God that even his shadow healed people.

How did Peter go from denying Jesus to being so full of God that his shadow healed people?

If we are honest, and this is the Truth lesson, so I hope we are, internally we want God to love us 100% and give us ALL of Himself but really, really, we do not want to love others like that. They just do not deserve it...

Our "me" nature is the most selfish nature out there. It is the biggest force and enemy that we, you and I, will have to deal with. We like to think that it is satan who is the biggest enemy, but satan actually uses your "me" factor against you on a regular basis. He just works with what is already there.

Self-Preservation. Peter had used his self-preservation the night Jesus was arrested. He denied Jesus and fled.

God will not force you to be 100% His. Just like He will not force salvation on anyone, they have to make their own choice. To have perfect "love" we will need to accept two things:

1) God is complete Love (all segments of the circle graph)
2) God can put His complete love into you: when you ask for the Holy Spirit to come and reside inside your heart. Get rid of the "me" rights inside of you. That means taking, demolishing getting rid of the blocks, wounds and the things we think are "our" rights.

Yes, *He has provided ALL you need. Everything in the Love Circle, Everything in the Daddy Circle. Everything.*

But He will not force you to take it. You, you must be the one who gets out of the way. The #1 block to not healing, not living the way God intended – is YOU.

Peter was very much human, he disowned Jesus 3 times the night Jesus was betrayed.

All the other disciples also ran for their lives; the "me" factor took over. They were scared and they ran.

And yet these very men, these very selfish men, were the ones who built the church, they were who God used to change the world. Jesus came back after His death and restored them.

What changed?

#1) They **saw** their dead Jesus standing there very much alive.

They saw a miracle; something that was totally impossible a super natural miracle. God got their attention with something they could not deny.

#2) They **had** heart changes; the Holy Spirit **came into** them and downloaded the Love

#3) They realized **whose they were.** After His resurrection Jesus restored the disciples. He never talked about their failure, He died for their failure. He talked about their future and what He expected them to do. He gave them new purpose and meaning – He told them how He sees them.

"Therefore go and make disciples of all nations, baptizing them in the name of the Father and of the Son and of the Holy Spirit."
Matthew 28:19

#4) They **went** from Dead to Life.

"We know that we have passed from death to life, because we love each other. Anyone who does not love remains in death."
1 John 3:14

Literally these fellows went from dead to life. They were so scared for their lives they ran, hid and were stopped. They were as good as dead, no ministry happening here. Jesus gave them new life, new purpose. After they saw Jesus, they realized there is no "death". Jesus proved once and for all that He is Life and we will never die, we go from life to life. There is something more, something bigger out there for us. Jesus is life and these fellows knew it!

"I am the way the truth and the life." John 14:6

When you give yourself 100% to God, whole hearted, then God will use you to change the world just like He did with the disciples when He restored them. He changed the world through a handful of selfish men that had already denied Him. He will do it with you by reminding you <u>who and whose you are.</u>

What will He do with you? That my friends is 100% truth.

End Song: *Voice of Truth* – Casting Crowns

Prayer: Pray and ask God to show you truth in your innermost parts, the parts that you have been hiding. Pray that you would be open to speaking in truth and love from this moment on. Give your self-preservation nature over to God, allow Him to take care of you, tell Him you are willing to let Him take over. Ask Him to give you the truth of who you are: how He sees you, what your purpose is. Prepare to be amazed my friends, because what God has for you "is" amazing.

Drawings, Doodles & Notes:

Drawings, Doodles & Notes:

Session 9: Conclusion -   What Does Love Look Like?

Recap

The past few weeks we have gone over Real versus Imitation Love, Daddies, Separation from God, Yourself, and Others. We saw that God talks about us, knows us. We have seen that Love costs and Love can hurt. We have acknowledged that Love and Truth go together, and that God knows our name. How can we sum that all up into a take away that we will remember? What would Real Love look like in a person's life…

❖

Mary the Mother of Jesus. Mary is a pregnant teenager, in a culture where out of wedlock pregnancies are met with death.

"I am the Lord's servant," Mary answered. "May your word to me be fulfilled." Then the angel left her." Luke 1:38

"And Mary said: "My soul glorifies the Lord and my spirit rejoices in God my Savior, for he has been mindful of the humble state of his servant. From now on all generations will call me blessed, for the Mighty One has done great things for me— holy is his name. His mercy extends to those who fear him, from generation to generation. He has performed mighty deeds with his arm; he has scattered those who are proud in their inmost thoughts. He has brought down rulers from their thrones but has lifted up the humble. He has filled the hungry with good things but has sent the rich away empty. He has helped his servant Israel, remembering to

be merciful to Abraham and his descendants forever, just as he

promised our ancestors."   Luke 1:46-55

Love is Spontaneous not Forced
Love is Impartation not Imitation
Love is a Delight not a Sacrifice
Love is not Good Doing it is God likeness
Love is A Life of Service
*Author Unknown

Mary decided that her life was the Lord's, He could have ALL of her and she delighted to do it for Him. Mary, when told this hard and confusing news of an unplanned pregnancy, wrote the above song of adoration and praise to God. Mary's sacrifice of her life had world changing ramifications. That is a life lived in Love. That is what Love looks like.

I am sure we have all heard many sermons on doing "works & service". I feel that we have often not been taught what "works" really are.

In our life we tend to separate "Christian activities" from the "everyday activities", we think that washing dishes, mopping the floor, going to work or watching the kids are separate from Christian "works" but Jesus NEVER separated any tasks.

Jesus whole life was an "act of service" whether He was eating, walking along the lake, teaching on the mountain or feeding the 5,000. Jesus was working the whole time, doing the will of His Father.

"Jesus gave them this answer: "Very truly I tell you, the Son can do nothing by himself; he can do only what he sees his Father doing, because whatever the Father does the Son also does." John 5:19

"I have not spoken on My own, but the Father who sent Me has commanded Me what to say and how to say it. And I know that His command leads to eternal life. So I speak exactly what the Father has told Me to say." John 12:49-50

"Jesus therefore said, 'When you lift up the Son of Man, then you will know that I am He, and I do nothing on My own initiative, but I speak these things as the Father taught Me.'" John 8:28

In our love circle, if we cannot separate or take anything out of it, why do we think we can separate our lives into secular and Christian? Our whole life is our circle. Jesus life was a life of whole devotion no matter what He was doing. Our lives should be the same, one complete unit, so that no matter if we are changing a baby, wiping a nose, shopping at the market or sitting at work or in a pew, all of our life will be our "Christian work".

Oswald Chambers says: *"Beware of anything that competes with your loyalty to Jesus Christ. The greatest competitor of true devotion to Jesus is the service we do for Him. It is easier to serve than to pour out our lives completely for Him."*[17]

God has only ever asked one thing from you: *"Love the Lord your God with all your heart, with all your mind and all your strength. Love you neighbor as yourself."* Matthew 22:37-39

If you do the first part the second comes naturally, only one thing is required: *"Love the Lord your God with all your heart, with all your mind and all your strength."*

---

[17] Oswald Chambers web quote: https://utmost.org/it-is-the-lord/

He does not command us to "work" and "do". **He commands us to Love.** We often get so focused on what we can or should "do" for God that we lose Him and the Love in the process.

Mary Magdalene was completely focused on God. Her life was lived as an example of what it means to follow Him whole heartedly.

David Jeremiah[18] says about Mary: *"People who receive a gift respond in different ways. Some act as if they deserved it, while others live in awe from then on that they were graced with such a treasure. The Christian's estimate of the value of the gift of salvation is measured by the level of gratitude in the response."*

I love this line: "The Christian's estimate of the value of the gift...is measured by the level of gratitude in the response." How much do we value God's gift of salvation to us?

Mary lived out her response with her life. Mary became a woman who loved (agape).

David Jeremiah did a remarkable history on Mary in his study Mary Magdalene:

Mary was one of the women that Jesus healed of seven demons. She was a woman with financial means (Luke 8:1-3). After meeting with Jesus she was transformed and freed from the demons (Ephesians 2). She was the follower of Jesus who was the very most grateful. She ministered to Jesus. She followed Him while on earth. She followed Him to the Cross. (Matthew 27:56, Mark 15:40) Even when the disciples had fled, she was with Him at His burial. She watched the tomb get sealed. (Matthew 27:61) She was the first to see the empty tomb. (Matthew 28:1, Mark 15:47). She was the first to see Jesus' resurrection. (Mark 16:12)

---

[18] David Jeremiah CD: http://www.davidjeremiah.org/shop/p-7276-mary-magdalene.aspx

She was the first to announce the empty tomb to Peter and John. She knew Jesus so intimately that He just spoke her name and she knew He was her Lord. Jesus appeared first to a woman - Mary Magdalene. Jesus told her to go proclaim the news. (John 20:17-18) The most important event of history and He showed Himself to a woman and told her to go tell the men.

Mary free from the demons that lived inside her, (which would have broken her, blocked her and hurt her) in her freedom she lived out her response with her life in an act of gratitude to God. She truly valued God's gift and she knew "whose" she was. She walked in freedom knowing her value and identity to God. Mary knew God.

We all have received Gods' gift of freedom. Jesus died to set us free from sins, He took them upon Himself.

How will you live out your gratitude? Thoughts:

Only one thing is needed, stay close to the source. Mary stayed close to the source. *"Love the Lord your God with all your heart, all your soul and all your mind."*   Matthew 22:37

When you are sourced in God, He will live through you.

Remember all the "I Wills" of session 3 we found in Ezekiel and Jeremiah? God will do the work.

He will love through you. He will work through you. It will not be you doing any of it. It will be your life lived out as a whole act of service to God.

God says *"I am the vine you are the branches"* John 15:5
Stay close to the source.

God says *"I am the shepherd you are the sheep"* John 10:14-15
Stay close to the source.

God says *"I am the bread of life – partake of my body"*
John 6:35,41 Stay close to the source.

God says *"I am the Way, the Truth and the Life – follow me"*
John 14:6   Stay close to the source.

Gods says *"I am the Living Water – drink from me."* John 4:14
Stay close to the source.

God says *"My Yoke is easy, my burden is light – abide in me."*
Matthew 11:30   Stay close to the source.

When you are sourced in God, _He will_ live through you. _He will_ love through you. _He will_ work through you. It will not be you doing any of it.

It will be impartation not imitation.

It will be a delight. It will be easy not forced. You will be the ground that produces a hundredfold crop.

"Behold, the sower went out to sow; and as he sowed, some seeds fell beside the road, and the birds came and ate them up. Others fell on the rocky places, where they did not have much soil; and immediately they sprang up, because they had no depth of soil. But when the sun had risen, they were scorched; and because they had no root, they withered away. Others fell among the thorns, and the thorns came up and choked them out. And others

136

fell on the good soil and yielded a crop, some a hundredfold, some sixty, and some thirty. He who has ears, let him hear." Matthew 13:3-9 (also found in Mark 4:3-8 and Luke 8:5-8)

Will you be ground that produces a crop, a hundred, sixty or thirty times what was sown?

We think we have the right to tell God where we want to be used. Staying close to the source alleviates that issue. We will be willing to be used wherever God places us, in whatever situation He puts us in, with whomever people He chooses, and we will be willing to be used by Him for His purposes and all we have to do is *STAY CLOSE TO THE SOURCE.*

God has given us His complete and Perfect Love, He gave us a New Heart and He did it for His glory.

God is asking us today the same question that Jesus asked Peter....

Jesus: Simon...do you love (*agape*) me more than these.
Peter: Yes, Lord; you know that I love (*phileo*) you.
Jesus: Simon...do you...love (*agape*) me?
Peter: Yes, Lord, you know that I love (*phileo*) you.
Jesus: Simon...do you love (*phileo*) me?
Peter: [Grieved] "Lord...you know that I love (*phileo*) you."
John 21:15-17

Jesus twice asked Peter, "Do you *agape* me?" [That is, are you willing to do things for my sake that you do not want to do?] Peter was not sure where he stood with Jesus, so he was trying to let Jesus know that he was still a true friend, and had *phileo* love for Jesus.

The third time Jesus spoke to Peter, he came to Peter's level and asked if Peter were indeed a true friend (*phileo*), which grieved

Peter. Jesus knew what Peter did not know. Jesus would be taken up into heaven, and Peter and the other disciples would be left to carry out His work on earth, which would require hardship. **We know love can be hard, it costs something.**

Let me ask you... if God said to you today, "Do you agape me?" what would be your response?

Read this passage again and insert your name instead of "Simon"...

Jesus: (Your name)...do you love (*agape*) me more than these.
You: Yes, Lord; you know that I love (*phileo*) you.
Jesus: (Your name)...do you...love (*agape*) me?
You: Yes, Lord, you know that I love (*phileo*) you.
Jesus: (Your name)...do you love (*phileo*) me?
You: [Grieved] "Lord...you know that I love (*phileo*) you."
John 21:15-17

Do not dismiss this question! It is the most piercing question that God can ever ask you.

We want to boldly claim that we love God just like Peter did the night before he denied him three times. But what does our inner nature say? It can only be discovered by asking ourselves this question.

If we are honest (and again I pray you will be), we will probably say back to God:

"Yes God I love (phileo) you."

We will state it as emotional love, just like Peter did. The love of a good friend, even a best friend because in reality we are scared of what He might ask of us. The great news is He has already given you ALL you need to handle anywhere He places you.

"For the Word of God is living and powerful... piercing even to the division of soul and spirit." Hebrews 4:12

It takes the Word of God to penetrate to the deep recesses of our soul and spirit, to break off our old inner man who is hanging on for self-preservation (and it is human nature to do so). There is no mistaking the pain that is caused by God when He points out our deceptions about ourselves, because He speaks Truth. It is at the exact moment the pain is felt that Truth is revealed and freedom comes.

Mary Magdalene Agaped Jesus. She stayed so close to her source that He used her mightily in His kingdom.

Mary, the mother of Jesus Agaped Jesus. She stayed so close to her source that He used her mightily in His Kingdom.

Your God, Your Daddy is looking for a family resemblance. We, who are parents, love it when someone says, "Oh he/she looks just like you."

Our heavenly Daddy loves it too.

"But to all who did receive him, who believed in his name, he gave the right to become children of God" John 1:12

"For in Christ Jesus you are all sons of God, through faith." Galatians 3:26

God wants us to have His family resemblance. He loves to hear someone say that we look or act like Him. God is love therefore so should we be.

He is looking for that one person out of a few who will give up their rights to themselves and allow Him to have total access to their life. That person will be the person who Agapes' God.

The Love of God is there because it has been poured into our hearts by the Holy Spirit.

"And hope does not put us to shame, because God's love has been poured out into our hearts through the Holy Spirit, who has been given to us." Romans 5:5

He wants it back.

Did you get that? God wants His love, poured into our hearts to love Him back with pure, agape love.

When we try to prove to God that we love Him it is a sign that we surely do not: because we human beings cannot love God in an Agape way. Agape Love is God Love. Only the Life of God can exhibit true, perfect, complete Love and that life comes to us in the Holy Spirit. Only Gods love is the true Pearl - the treasure our hearts were created and long for.

Remember God never asks us for something that He Himself is not willing to give. In asking us to totally surrender to Him, He already set the example. He did that for us.

Did you study biology in school – the water cycle of the planet?

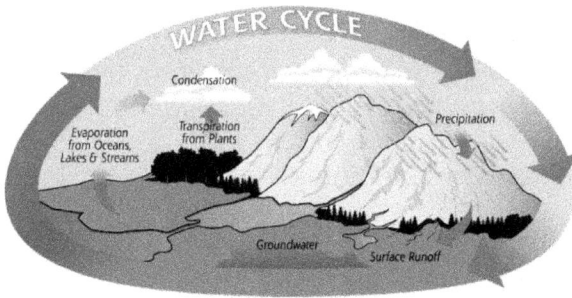

19

Water forms in the clouds and then it drops in the form of rain, snow or hail onto the earth to water it and make things grow. That water goes into streams, lakes and the ocean, the air then soaks up the water in the form of evaporation and puts it back into the sky and into the clouds where it waits until it is dropped again on to the earth, forming a "water circle".

God has His own eco system: God gave us His Agape love and He wants us to Agape love ourselves and other people with the Agape love He gave us so that His people would Agape love Him back.

©2016 Jane Wheeler

God poured His love onto man gave him a new heart, put His Holy Spirit inside of us to love and to love Him back.

A Perfect Complete Love Circle.

"Therefore say to the Israelites, 'This is what the Sovereign LORD

---

[19] https://pmm.nasa.gov/education/water-cycle

says: It is not for your sake, people of Israel, that I am going to do these things, but for the sake of my holy name, which you have profaned among the nations where you have gone." Ezekiel 36:22

God says repeatedly in the Bible that He will not share His glory with another.

"I am the LORD; that is my name! I will not yield my glory to another or my praise to idols." Isaiah 42:8

"For my own sake, for my own sake, I do this. How can I let myself be defamed? I will not yield my glory to another." Hebrews 48:11

It is for His glory.

When the circle is complete then we will be One with the Father as Jesus was One with His Father thus making the circle complete and forming a *Complete Love Circle.*

We will be totally free and real, no imitation, no plastic, and the byproduct of your life will be influencing the world around you as you live your daily life totally devoted and abiding in God. Free to walk as the person God sees and says you to be. You will have the ability to change the world. You will be the person who makes a difference. You will have no separation from God, Yourself or Others. You will be walking in truth and love.

God is asking you today – Do You Agape Me?

Put down your fear, get rid of your I and me's (selfishness), let go of your rights, and walk into freedom knowing **who and whose** you are, because apart from salvation it will be the greatest gift you ever get.

What will your answer be...?

End Song: *No Longer Slaves: I Am A Child of God*, W. A. Zamorano, Bethel Music

Prayer: Prayerfully tell God what your answer is to His question: Do you Agape Me? Pray that you are willing to be that one person who will change the world around you. Ask God to complete His Complete Love Circle in your body and life.

Drawings, Doodles & Notes:

Drawings, Doodles & Notes:

Drawings, Doodles & Notes:

Drawings, Doodles & Notes:

About the Author:

Jane Wheeler lives in the oil town of Grande Prairie, Northern Alberta, Canada with her husband and two golden retrievers. Jane has three grown sons that bring joy, excitement and sometimes lots of prayer to her life.

Together with her husband they create amazing wood furniture and other treasures in their little woodshop.

God sees Jane as a teacher, leader, writer and builder. When she is physically not building in the woodshop, you will find her building into the Kingdom by teaching, leading and writing as God leads and directs her.

You can connect with her on her website where you will find her contact page, and a link to her weekly Wednesday Blog: *Midweek Moments* plus a list of other resources she has available.

If you wish to sign up to get her weekly blog emailed to you – please send a note on the contact page.

Website: http://www.rayofsunshineministries.com

www.ingramcontent.com/pod-product-compliance
Lightning Source LLC
Chambersburg PA
CBHW072004060426
42446CB00042B/1813